D1587007

BrightRED Study Guide

CfE HIGHER

MUSIC

Adrian Finnerty

First published in 2019 by:
Bright Red Publishing Ltd
1 Torphichen Street
Edinburgh
EH3 8HX

A CIP record for this book is available from the British Library.

ISBN 978-1-84948-320-9

With thanks to:
PDQ Digital Media Solutions Ltd, Bungay (layout), Sue Lyons (copy-edit).
Cover design and series book design by Caleb Rutherford – e i d e t i c.

Acknowledgements
Every effort has been made to seek all copyright-holders. If any have been overlooked, then Bright Red Publishing will be delighted to make the necessary arrangements.

Permission has been sought from all relevant copyright holders and Bright Red Publishing are grateful for the use of the following:

Heinrich Klaffs/Creative Commons (CC BY-SA 2.0)[1] (p 6); Alatele fr/Creative Commons (CC BY-SA 2.0)[1] (p 6); Ice Boy Tell/Creative Commons (CC BY-SA 4.0)[2] (p 7); Atamari/Creative Commons (CC BY-SA 4.0)[2] (p 7); Vincent Lock/Creative Commons (CC BY 2.0)[3] (p 9); Caleb Rutherford (p 9); Library of Congress, Prints & Photographs Division, Carl Van Vechten Collection, [reproduction number, LC-USZ62-103977] (p 10); Image from 'The Magic Flute' © Opera San José, photo by Pat Kirk (p 15); Francisco Peralta Torrejon/Creative Commons (CC BY-SA 4.0)[2] (p 15); GDJ/Pixabay (p 20); Dave Conner/Creative Commons (CC BY 2.0)[3] (p 20); Caleb Rutherford (p 24); Library of Congress, Prints & Photographs Division, George Grantham Bain Collection [reproduction number LC-DIG-ggbain-32392] (p 27); Music score for Agnus Dei by Stravinsky © Copyright 1948 by Hawkes & Son (London) Ltd. (p 27); Estonian Foreign Ministry/Creative Commons (CC BY 2.0)[3] (p 49); Lanttuloora/Creative Commons (CC BY-SA 3.0)[4] (p 50); Serge Lido/Creative Commons (CC BY-SA 3.0)[4] (p 52); Music score for Kontakte by Stockhausen © Stockhausen-Stiftung für Musik, www.karlheinzstockhausen.org. Used with permission (p 52); Images licensed by Ingram Image (pp 56, 61, 64, 65, 68, 69, 72, 75, 78, 79, 85, 88, 89); Caleb Rutherford Design (p 75); Paulnorthyorks/Creative Commons (CC BY-SA 4.0)[2] (p 79); Mariana Vusiatytska/Unsplash (p 86); scholacantorum/Pixabay (p 87); SteveAllenPhoto/iStock.com (p 90).

[1](CC BY-SA 2.0) http://creativecommons.org/licenses/by-sa/2.0/

[2](CC BY-SA 4.0) http://creativecommons.org/licenses/by-sa/4.0/

[3](CC BY 2.0) http://creativecommons.org/licenses/by/2.0/

[4](CC BY-SA 3.0) https://creativecommons.org/licenses/by-sa/3.0/

Printed and bound in the UK.

CONTENTS

INTRODUCTION

COURSE OVERVIEW

INTRODUCTION

The aims of the Higher Music course are to enable you to:

- broaden your knowledge and understanding of music and musical literacy by listening to music and learning to recognise, and distinguish, level specific music concepts, signs and symbols used in music notation

- experiment with, and use, music concepts in creative ways, using compositional methods to compose original music and self-reflect on your creative choices

- develop performing skills on two instruments, or one instrument and voice, through regular practice and self-reflection.

Throughout the Higher Music course, you will develop a range of musical skills, knowledge and understanding. These will include:

- skills in listening to music to promote aural perception and discrimination

- knowledge and understanding of music styles, concepts, notation signs and symbols

- skills in creating original music using compositional methods

- reviewing the creative process and evaluating your own composing

- skills in performing music in contrasting styles on two contrasting instruments, or one instrument and voice

- self-reflection and review of your rehearsal and practice skills.

COURSE CONTENT

The Higher Music course has an integrated approach to learning about music. It combines practical activities in performing and composing with music literacy and listening to music. Learning about a wide range of music concepts is central to the course. Throughout the course, you will have opportunities to draw upon your understanding of music styles and concepts as you experiment with these in creative ways when performing and creating music.

Higher Music concepts

The music concepts are all the styles, music features and terms that you will learn about as part of your Higher Music course. You will explore these concepts in a variety of ways through listening to music, creating your own music and performing music.

The concepts in the Higher Music course build on previous knowledge and understanding of music concepts at lower levels. This means that you will be expected to have a secure understanding of the music concepts at National 3, National 4 and National 5 levels, in addition to knowledge and understanding of the Higher Music concepts.

The tables below lists all the concepts that are introduced at Higher level. All the concepts for National 3, National 4 and National 5 Music can be found in the Bright Red N5 Music Study Guide.

contd

Music Concepts: CfE Higher

Styles	Melody/harmony	Rhythm/tempo	Texture/structure/form	Timbre
Plainchant	Mode or modal	3 against 2	Basso continuo	Tremolando
Oratorio	Relative major	Time changes	Concerto grosso	Harmonics
Mass	Relative minor	Irregular time signatures	Ritornello	String quartet
Recitative	Interval	Triplets	Passacaglia	Ripieno
Sonata	Obligato	Augmentation	Da capo aria	Concertino
Chamber music	Acciaccatura	Diminution	Sonata form	Coloratura
String quartet	Mordent		Exposition	
Lied	Plagal cadence		Subject	
Impressionist	Interrupted cadence		Through-composed	
Musique concrète	Tierce de Picardie			
Jazz funk	Dominant 7th			
Soul music	Diminished triad			
	Diminished 7th			
	Added 6th			
	Harmonic minor scale			
	Melodic minor scale			

Music literacy

Melody/harmony	Rhythm/tempo	Texture/structure/form	Dynamics/timbre
Bass clef: E–C (range of notes from E below the stave to middle C)	Quavers, crotchets, dotted crotchets and dotted minims within	Phrase mark	Accents (>)
Transposing from treble clef down one octave into bass clef	$\frac{6}{8}$ $\frac{9}{8}$ $\frac{12}{8}$ time		Slurs
Identifying chords I, IV, V and VI in major and minor keys in treble and bass clefs	Triplet quavers, triplet crotchets		Staccato (.)
Identifying tonic, subdominant and dominant notes in the keys of C, G and F major and A minor	Rests: quaver, crotchet, dotted crotchet, minim, semibreve, whole bar		
Naming diatonic intervals: 2nd, 3rd, 4th, 5th, 6th, 7th and octave	Da capo (D.C.)		
Writing diatonic intervals above a given note in treble clef			

DON'T FORGET

For the Higher Music course, you will also need to know all the music concepts for National 3, National 4 and National 5.

THINGS TO DO AND THINK ABOUT

Remember to:

- reflect regularly on your performing progress
- review and evaluate your composing.

Use the tables above as a checklist of the Higher concepts you need to know. You could highlight the concepts in different colours, choosing a different colour for each theme or topic. This will help you to identify all the concepts that you already know, and let you see which concepts you might not be so sure of.

Create a mind map for each theme or topic that you study, showing which concepts relate to that theme.

POPULAR MUSIC

SOUL AND JAZZ FUNK

You will already have learned about a number of popular music styles as part of the National 5 Music course.

These included popular music styles from early in the twentieth century such as Blues, Gospel, Ragtime, Jazz and Swing, and styles that emerged during the second half of the twentieth century, including Rock'n'roll, Rock, Pop, Reggae, Rap and Celtic Rock.

If you want to revise popular music styles from previous levels, you can refer to the Bright Red N5 Music Study Guide, and also go to www.brightredbooks.net/subjects/n5music.

For Higher Music there are two additional popular music styles that you also need to be aware of: **Soul music** and **Jazz funk.**

Ray Charles (1930–2004)

SOUL MUSIC

Soul music (usually referred to just as **Soul**) is a popular music style that originated in the USA in the late 1950s and early 1960s. Associated with record labels such as *Tamala Motown*, *Atlantic* and *Stax*, soul music incorporates elements of Gospel music, Rhythm and Blues, and Jazz.

Soul music was made popular by a number of black American performers including Ray Charles, Marvin Gaye, James Brown, Otis Redding and Aretha Franklin.

Important characteristics of Soul music include an emphasis on vocals, conveying strong emotions, intensity of feeling and an impassioned performance. Other features that are sometimes present include call and response (or question and answer) between the lead vocalist and the backing singers, and some elements of improvisation.

Marvin Gaye (1939–1984)

James Brown (1933–2006)

Otis Redding (1941–1967)

Aretha Franklin (1942–2018)

Example:

Listen to Aretha Franklin singing *Respect* on the Digital Zone.

As you listen to the song, note the following musical features:

- introduction featuring saxophones, electric guitar and drum kit
- solo female voice, conveying strong emotions
- backing vocals
- question and answer between soloist and backing vocals
- instrumental section, featuring saxophones
- saxophone solo, featuring improvisation
- solo female voice, with backing vocals
- saxophones join in towards the end.

VIDEO LINK

Listen to examples of classic Soul performances at www.brightredbooks.net

6

JAZZ FUNK

Herbie Hancock (b. 1940)

Jazz funk is a popular music style that emerged in the USA in 1970s. It proved to be most popular throughout the 1970s and the early 1980s.

Jazz funk is a combination of Jazz improvisation with elements of Rock and Funk.

Common features of Jazz funk include the use of amplified instruments such as synthesizers, electric guitars, bass guitar and drum kit, along with Funk influenced bass lines and the driving rhythms and character of Rock.

In the 1970s many American Jazz musicians, including Herbie Hancock, combined Jazz, Funk and Rock elements.

Example:

Listen to *Cantelope Island* performed by Herbie Hancock on the Digital Zone.

As you listen to the music, note the following musical features:

- introduction featuring a riff played on the piano
- drum kit and bass double bass join in
- electric guitar joins in and plays an improvised solo
- extended piano solo with improvisation
- electric guitar returns with an improvised solo.

In the late 1970s and early 1980s British groups, such as Shakatak, began to explore Jazz funk, softening the hard-edged rhythms of Funk and incorporating more Jazz and Rock elements.

Shakatak

Example:

Listen to – *Easier Said Than Done* by Shakatak.

As you listen to the music, note the following musical features:

- female vocals
- accompanying instruments include electric guitar, bass guitar, piano and drum kit
- piano solos featuring improvisation
- instrumental break featuring synthesiser.

 THINGS TO DO AND THINK ABOUT

Consider some of the main similarities and differences between Jazz and Jazz funk.

 **DON'T FORGET**

Jazz funk incorporates Jazz improvisation with elements of Rock.

 VIDEO LINK

Listen to the tracks for the activities in this section on the Digital Zone.

 ONLINE TEST

Test yourself on popular music styles at www.brightredbooks.net

7

OTHER POPULAR MUSIC CONCEPTS

There are other musical features that are common in different styles of popular music. These include the use of different types of chords, as well as different playing techniques.

CHORDS: ADDED 6TH, DOMINANT 7TH AND DIMINISHED 7TH

As the name suggests, an **added 6th** chord is a basic three note chord with the 6th note above the root added. For example, if you look at the three basic chords of C, F and G, they each contain three notes – the root, the third and the 5th.

If you then added the 6th note from the root to each of these chords this would create added 6th chords.

The added 6th chord is slightly richer and sweeter sounding, and is often used in Jazz and other styles of popular music.

A **dominant 7th** chord is a basic three-note chord with the lowered 7th note above the root added.

Strictly speaking, a dominant 7th would be based on the dominant (or 5th) note of a scale and is sometimes written using the Roman numeral V7. For example, in the key of C major the dominant 7th chord would be G7 because G is the dominant (i.e. 5th) note of the C major scale.

In various styles of popular music, however, it is not uncommon to have 7ths added to other chords as well.

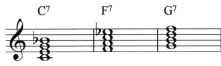

A **diminished** chord consists of two intervals of a minor 3rd built on top of each other.

Here are the chords E diminished, B diminished and G sharp diminished, using common abbreviations:

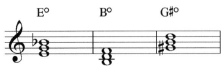

A **diminished 7th** chord consists of three intervals of a minor 3rd built one on top of each other, the interval between the lower and upper note being a diminished 7th. Here are the chords E diminished 7th, B diminished 7th and G sharp diminished 7th, using common abbreviations:

HARMONICS

Harmonics are the very high notes produced on a stringed instrument by lightly touching the strings at certain points. On a guitar these can sound *bell-like*.

Relative minor

The minor key which is related to a major key and shares the same key signature is called the **relative minor**. A song, or a piece of music, in a major key will sometime modulate to the relative minor, as this is its most closely related minor key.

A number of popular songs start in a major key and then modulate to the relative minor key. *Listen to When I'm Sixty-Four* and *We Can Work It Out* by The Beatles. Both songs are in a major key, but have a middle 8 section that modulates to the relative minor key.

Relative major

The major key which is related to a minor key and shares the same key signature is called the **relative major**. A song, or piece of music, in a minor key will sometimes modulate to the relative major, as this is its most closely related major key.

The popular song *My Funny Valentine*, Latin American classic *Tico Tico*, and the Jazz standard *Harlem Nocturne* all start in a minor key and modulate to the relative major key.

VIDEO LINK

Listen to examples of harmonics played on the guitar at www.brightredbooks.net

VIDEO LINK

You can listen to the tracks mentioned in this spread on the Bright Red Digital Zone.

ONLINE TEST

Test yourself on popular music styles at www.brightredbooks.net

THINGS TO DO AND THINK ABOUT

If you listen to the four strings of a ukulele, notice that they are tuned to the notes contained in an added 6th chord (C, E, G and A)

Experiment with different added 6th, dominant 7th, diminished and diminished 7th chords, and consider how you might incorporate any of them into your own composition.

Listen to any song from a style of your choice. Create a *song plan,* identifying the main sections of the song, such as introduction, **verse, chorus, middle 8** and **coda**.

Within your *song plan*, try to identify any other prominent features, such as the instruments being played or any other melodic or harmonic features such as added 6th, 7th or diminished chords.

9

IRREGULAR TIME SIGNATURES

Irregular time signatures are time signatures that do not fit into the usual pattern of simple or compound time. Rather than having two, three or four beats in every bar, irregular time signatures might have five or seven beats in each bar.

Composers and performers of different styles of music have made interesting use of irregular time signatures.

Paul Desmond (1924–1977)

TAKE FIVE

A popular Jazz piece that features an irregular time signature is *Take Five* by the American saxophone player and composer Paul Desmond.

One of the most significant features of *Take Five* is that it has five beats in every bar.

As you listen to *Take Five*, note the following musical features:

- introduction – riff played on the piano
- irregular time signature – five beats in a bar
- the piano is joined by the double bass and drum kit
- saxophone solo
- sequences
- saxophone, accompanied by piano, double bass and drum kit
- improvised solo on the saxophone
- improvised solo on the piano.

VIDEO LINK

Listen to *Take Five* by Paul Desmond, performed by Paul Desmond on saxophone with the Dave Brubeck Quartet on the Digital Zone.

The Dave Brubeck Quartet

UNSQUARE DANCE

Another Jazz piece that uses an irregular time signature is *Unsquare Dance* by the American Jazz pianist and composer Dave Brubeck. Although based on a Blues structure, one of the most significant features of *Unsquare Dance* is that it has seven beats in every bar.

Listen to *Unsquare Dance* by Dave Brubeck, performed by the Dave Brubeck Quartet.

As you listen to *Unsquare Dance*, note the following musical features:

- introduction – riff played the double bass and hand claps
- irregular time signature – seven beats in a bar

contd

- descending phrases played on the piano
- a melody played on the piano featuring **acciaccaturas** (grace notes), triplets and syncopation

- a drum kit solo featuring rim shots (a playing technique in which the drum stick strikes the rim and the head of the drum simultaneously)
- piano solo
- coda
- the music finishes with a perfect cadence.

IRREGULAR TIME SIGNATURES IN ROCK MUSIC

Irregular time signatures have also been used in other styles of popular music, including Rock. The Song *Money*, from the album *Dark Side of The Moon*, by the British Progressive Rock band Pink Floyd, uses an irregular time signature. Composed by the band's bass player Roger Waters, *Money* has seven beats in the bar for most of the song.

The very start of the song also uses **Musique Concrète** techniques, in that it features recorded money-related sound effects such as the ringing of a cash register and the jingling of coins. These sound effects also appear at other points in the song.

Pink Floyd

Example:

Listen to *Money* by Pink Floyd.

As you listen, note the following musical features:

- musique concrète techniques – ringing of a cash register and jingling of coins
- riff played by the bass guitar

- irregular time signature – seven beats in a bar
- drum kit and electric guitar join in
- solo male vocalist
- saxophone solo
- time signature changes to simple quadruple time (four beats in the bar)
- electric guitar solo
- time signature changes back to seven beats in the bar
- return to the open bass guitar riff, along with solo male vocalist
- the music fades out.

 THINGS TO DO AND THINK ABOUT

Listen to songs or instrumental pieces from different styles and try to identify any that feature irregular time signatures or time changes.

VOCAL MUSIC

RECITATIVE

VOCAL MUSIC: INTRODUCTION

Vocal music is any kind of music performed by one or more singers, with or without instrumental accompaniment.

Female voices are generally divided into three main types: soprano, mezzo-soprano, and alto (also known as contralto).

Male voices are also generally divided into three main types: tenor, baritone, and bass.

A choir is a group of singers. Choirs can be of any size (large or small), containing any combination of voices, and performing music in any style.

The most common type of choir contains mixed voices (i.e. a mixture of male and female voices). The four main types of voice that form the basis of a standard mixed choir are soprano, alto, tenor and bass, often referred to by the initials SATB for short.

You will already be familiar with a number of concepts associated with vocal music as these have been covered at N5 level.

If you want to revise concepts from previous levels, you can refer to the *BrightRED National 5 Music Study Guide*.

For Higher Music, the additional vocal concepts that you will need to be familiar with are **Recitative**, **Da capo aria**, **Coloratura**, **Lied** and **Through-composed**.

Vocal styles such as oratorio, plainchant and mass are dealt with more thoroughly in the chapter on Sacred music.

RECITATIVE

A **recitative** is a type of vocal music (often found in operas and oratorios) in which the singer follows the natural rhythm of speech. Recitatives are used in operas and oratorios to move the story or plot on, usually leading into an aria or a chorus.

There are two main types of recitative:

- *Recitativo secco* ('dry' recitative) is a type of recitative in which the singer follows the natural rhythm of speech. It is usually syllabic and has a simple chordal accompaniment provided by basso continuo (cello and harpsichord).

- *Recitativo accompagnato* or *recitativo stromentato* ('accompanied' recitative) would have a stricter rhythm and is more song-like. It is often more melismatic and would be accompanied by other instruments, sometimes an orchestra.

Example:

A good example of *recitativo secco* is the recitative *Thy hand Belinda* from the opera *Dido and Aeneas* by Purcell. Dido (Queen of Carthage) is heartbroken that Aeneas (a Trojan Prince) is leaving her. He then says he will stay after all, but Dido will have none of it. As Aeneas heads for his ship, Dido sings the recitative *Thy hand Belinda* . . .

Listen to the recitative *Thy hand Belinda* from the opera *Dido and Aeneas* by Purcell while following the printed music. The harpsichord player creates a chordal accompaniment to the voice, elaborating on the chords indicated by the *figured bass* and a cello plays the basso continuo line. This is an example of *recitativo secco*.

contd

12

As you listen to the music, note the following features:

- the melody is sung by an alto
- the tonality is minor
- the voice is accompanied by a harpsichord and basso continuo
- the voice part follows the natural rhythm of the words, indicating this is a recitative
- there is a melisma on the word 'darkness'
- the recitative ends with an imperfect cadence.

Example:

Listen to the recitative *Thus saith the Lord* from the oratorio *Messiah* by Handel. The opening of the recitative is printed below. This is an example of *recitativo accompagnato*.

As you listen to the opening of the music, note the following features:

- the music starts with strings, playing a rising arpeggio
- the strings also play a dotted rhythm
- a bass voice is singing
- there is a melisma on the word 'shake'.

ACTIVITY

Listen to the whole recitative *Thus saith the Lord* while following the guide to the music in the table below. The text is printed in the left-hand column. The musical features are printed in the right-hand column at the point where they occur in the music. Try to identify the features as you listen to the music.

Thus saith the Lord,	1. Bass voice	the earth, the sea,	11.
the Lord of Hosts;	2. Dotted rhythm played by the strings	the dry land, all nations,	12.
		I'll shake; and the desire	13. Melisma
Yet once a little while	3.	of all nations shall come.	14.
and I will shake	4. Melisma	The Lord, whom ye seek,	15.
the heav'ns and the earth,	5.	shall suddenly come to His temple,	16.
the sea and the dry land;	6.		
And I will shake,	7. Melisma	even the messenger of the Covenant,	17.
and I will shake	8. Melisma and sequence		
all nations,	9. Repeated notes played by the strings	whom ye delight in:	18.
		behold, He shall come,	19.
I'll shake the heav'ns,	10.	Saith the Lord of Hosts.	20. Perfect cadence

THINGS TO DO AND THINK ABOUT

Consider the main differences between a recitative and an aria.

DA CAPO ARIA AND COLORATURA

DA CAPO ARIA

An aria is a solo song from an opera or oratorio, usually accompanied by an orchestra.

A **da capo aria** is an aria in ternary form (meaning that it has three sections – ABA). The first section (A1) would be performed by the singer exactly as it is written. The second section (B) would generally be a contrast, possibly being in a different key or having a different mood. The third section (A2) would be a repeat of section A1. However, rather than the music being written out again, the composer would simply write the performance direction 'da capo' (an Italian term that literally means 'from the head'), meaning to back to the beginning and repeat the first section in full.

The singer would often vary or embellish the melody during the third section, to make it sound more interesting and not just an exact repeat of the first section. The da capo aria is very common in operas and oratorios.

The aria *Lascia ch'io pianga* from the opera *Rinaldo* by Handel is an example of a da capo aria. The story of *Rinaldo* takes place in Jerusalem during the first crusades in the 11th century. Almirena, the daughter of Goffredo (Captain General of the Christian Army) is in love with Rinaldo (a Christian hero). Almirena is held prisoner by Argante (the Saracen king of Jerusalem) who also discloses his love for her. Mourning her captive state, Almirena sings the aria *Lascia ch'io pianga* (*Let me weep*).

DON'T FORGET

A da capo aria is in ternary (ABA) form, with section B being a contrasting section. The singer would then vary or embellish the melody on the return to section A.

DA CAPO (D.C.)

Da capo is an Italian term indicating that the performer should repeat a piece of music from the beginning. The abbreviation **D.C.** is often used.

 **ACTIVITY**

Listen to the aria *Lascia ch'io pianga* from the opera *Rinaldo* by Handel while following the guide to the music.

Introduction
- Strings
- Homophonic texture
- Major tonality
- Three beats in the bar

Section A1
- Soprano solo, starting as follows:

- Strings repeat the first four bars

Section B
- Soprano solo
- Basso continuo only (harpsichord or organ with cello)
- Minor tonality – relative minor key

Section A2
- Repeat of section A1
- Soprano solo
- Major tonality
- Soprano adds ornamentation to embellish the melody
- Strings finish with a repeat the opening section

ACTIVITY

Listen to the following examples of da capo arias from the oratorio *Messiah* by Handel:

1. *He was despised*

2. *The trumpet shall sound*

In each case:

- identify the type of voice singing
- consider how section B contrasts with section A
- listen to how the singer embellishes the melody when section A returns.

Opera San José resident artist Isabella Ivy as The Queen of the Night

COLORATURA

A **coloratura** is a type of operatic voice that features florid ornamentation, elaborate melodic decoration and agile virtuosic runs. Although the term coloratura can be applied to any type of voice, it is most often associated with the soprano.

A popular example of an aria for coloratura soprano is the *Queen of the Night Aria* from the opera *The Magic Flute* by Mozart: *Der Hölle Rache kocht in meinem Herzen* (*Hell's revenge burns in my heart*). *The Magic Flute* is an opera in two acts. It is a fairy tale story with themes of love and of good versus evil. The aria depicts the evil *Queen of the Night* in a fit of vengeful rage. She places a knife into the hand of her daughter Pamina and urges her to kill Sarastro, the Queen's rival, threatening to disown Pamina if she does not co-operate.

Example:

Listen to the *Queen Of The Night Aria* from the opera *The Magic Flute* by Mozart.
As you listen to the *Queen of the Night Aria*, try to identify the following features of the music:

- soprano solo
- accompanied by an orchestra
- aria from an opera
- a wide vocal range with high *tessitura*
- very agile and florid singing

- melismas
- sequences
- minor tonality
- perfect cadences.

Another example of a coloratura aria is *Sempre Libera* (*Always Free*), sung by the character Violetta at the end of Act 1 of the opera *La Traviata* by Verdi.

THINGS TO DO AND THINK ABOUT

Listen to the aria *Sempre Libera* (*Always Free*) from the opera *La Traviata* by Verdi.

Consider which musical features of this aria make it an example of coloratura singing.

VIDEO LINK

Listen to the tracks for this spread on the Digital Zone.

DON'T FORGET

Coloratura is term to describe high, florid singing.

ONLINE TEST

Test yourself on vocal music on the Digital Zone.

15

LIED 1

Lied (pronounced 'leed') is the German word for song. The plural is Lieder (songs)

The terms Lied and Lieder are generally used to refer to songs for voice and piano by 19th century German and Austrian composers of the Romantic period. Two composers particularly associated with composing Lieder are Schubert and Schumann

Franz Schubert (1797–1828)

Robert Schumann (1810–1856)

FRANZ SCHUBERT AND ROBERT SCHUMANN

Schubert was an Austrian composer who is regarded as the first important composer of Lieder. He composed over six hundred songs and was one of the first composers to treat the voice and piano as equal partners. The piano accompaniment would often establish the mood of the song, e.g. evoking the character of a rippling brook, a stormy morning, a moonlit night, or a whirring spinning-wheel.

Schumann was a German composer who composed over two hundred songs. Schumann's piano accompaniments are particularly rich and imaginative, and much of the musical and dramatic interest is carried by the piano. His songs often end with a coda for the piano on its own.

The structure or form of a Lied would depend on the text of the poem being set. Many examples of Lieder are in strophic form (i.e. the same music would be repeated for each verse). Some examples of Lieder are in ternary (ABA) form, in which the middle (B) section provides some musical contrast, possibly by being in a different key or having a different mood. Other examples of Lieder, however, are **through-composed**. This is a form in which there is little or no musical repetition. Sometimes small sections of the music might be repeated, but not complete verses. The composer allows the words of the poem to determine the structure of the music.

Both Schubert and Schumann, as well as other composers, also wrote *song-cycles*: collections of songs based on poems by the same poet, linked together by a theme, sometimes conveying a complete story.

You will now have the opportunity to listen to some examples of Lieder by Schubert and Schumann.

Example:

Listen to *An die Musik (To Music)* by Schubert while following the guide to the music.
The song is a tribute to the art of music, and is one of Schubert's the best-known songs.

Introduction
- The music begins with simple repeated chords played by the piano
- The left hand of the piano hints at the vocal melody to follow
- The tonality is major

contd

Verse 1
- The voice enters with the words *Du holde Kunst (You noble art):*

Du hol - de Kunst, in wie - viel grau - en— Stun- den,

wo mich des Le - bens wil - der Kreis um - strickt,

- The piano continues to play repeating chords in the accompaniment
- The verse ends with a short interlude played by the piano on its own

Verse 2
- The voice enters with the words *Oft hat ein Seufzer, deiner Harf' entflossen (Often has a sigh flowing out from your harp)*
- The melody of verse 2 is a repeat of the melody from verse 1
- The song is in trophic form (i.e. the same music is repeated for each verse)

Coda
- The piano rounds off the song with a short coda, based on the interlude heard at the end of verse 1.

In most examples of Lieder, the piano is not merely an accompaniment. The voice and piano are treated as equals, and the piano is often used to create the mood and character.

DER STÜRMISCHE MORGEN (THE STORMY MORNING)

Listen to another song by Schubert: *Der stürmische morgen (The stormy morning).*

This comes from a *song-cycle* called *Winterreise (Winter Journey)*, which is made up of twenty-four songs. As you listen, consider how Schubert captures the mood and character of a stormy morning.

Introduction

- The song begins with a dramatic introduction played by the piano

- It starts with a rising sequence

- The right and left hands are playing in octaves

- After another flourish of semiquavers there is a sforzando diminished 7th chord

- The quavers are played staccato and some of the semiquavers are accented

- Then there are two groups of triplets followed by a perfect cadence

- The tonality is minor

 THINGS TO DO AND THINK ABOUT

Listen again to the two verses of *An die Musik (To Music)* by Schubert. Try to describe the mood and character of the song, and consider how the piano accompaniment contributes to this mood and character.

 VIDEO LINK

Listen to the tracks for this spread on the Digital Zone.

DON'T FORGET

A lied is a German song in which the voice and piano are equally important.

 ONLINE TEST

Test yourself on vocal music on the Digital Zone.

17

LIED 2

DON'T FORGET

Lied is a song for voice and piano from the Romantic period. The piano accompaniment often helps to create the mood and character of the song.

THE STORMY MORNING (CONTD)

Verse 1

- The voice and piano are in unison / octaves
- The melody has a number of dotted rhythms and some wide leaps

Interlude

- After the first verse there is short interlude played on the piano
- This includes a descending triplet figure based on diminished chords
- The interlude ends with a perfect cadence

ONLINE

Head to www.brightredbooks.net to find the pieces mentioned in this topic, online activities, tests and more!

Verse 2

- The piano accompaniment is now homophonic (in block chords)
- The tonality is major

DON'T FORGET

Strophic is a form in which the same music is repeated for each verse. Through-composed is a form in which there is little or no musical repetition in the verses.

Verse 3

- The first line of the melody is based on the second line of the melody from verse 1
- The voice and piano are in unison / octaves
- The melody then continues differently
- The piano plays repeated chords at this point

DON'T FORGET

Find out more about diminished and diminished 7th chords in the Music Literacy section.

Coda

- The piano brings the song to a close with a repeat of the music from the interlude
- This includes a descending triplet figure based on diminished chords
- The music ends with a perfect cadence

Although part of the melody from verse 1 is used in verse 2, the music for the whole verse was not repeated. The composer allowed the words of the poem to determine the structure of the music. This means that the overall structure of the song is through-composed.

contd

WIDMUNG (DEDICATION)

Listen to *Widmung* (*Dedication*) by Schumann while following the guide to the music.

The title *Widmung* can be translated either as *Dedication* or *Devotion*. This is the first of a collection of twenty-six songs called *Myrthen* (*Myrtles*) that Schumann composed as a wedding gift for his wife, Clara. Myrtles are evergreen shrubs with white or rosy flowers that are often used to make bridal bouquets.

Introduction

- The song opens with a very short but lively introduction played by the piano
- The opening figure is based on an arpeggio pattern
- Although the rhythm is based mainly on grouped quavers, there is also a dotted rhythm
- The tonality is major

Section A1

- A soprano voice enters singing the first verse
- The joyful melody is sometimes doubled in the piano accompaniment
- The piano accompaniment is based on arpeggio patterns, and dotted notes, similar to the introduction
- The verse ends with a perfect cadence

Section B

- The mood is much calmer
- There is a change of key but the tonality is still major
- The vocal melody is more sustained, with longer notes
- The piano accompaniment is now based on repeated chords
- The repeated piano chords play a triplet rhythm
- The key changes back to the original key towards the end of this section
- The melody at this point is similar to part of section A
- The piano accompaniment returns to arpeggio patterns and dotted notes, similar to section A
- The piano plays a pedal note in the bass

Section A2

- There is a return to the melody and words of the first section
- The melody is again sometimes doubled in the piano accompaniment
- The piano accompaniment is based on arpeggio patterns and dotted notes
- The melody is altered towards the end

Coda

- The solo piano finishes the song with an expressive phrase which is played twice
- There is a ritardando at the end

THINGS TO DO AND THINK ABOUT

Listen to the some examples of Lieder on the Digital Zone and identify the type of voice singing, decide if the structure of the song is ternary form, strophic or through-composed, and consider how the piano accompaniment contributes to the overall mood and character of the song.

SACRED MUSIC

INTRODUCTION

From the earliest times, music has played an important part in the lives of different communities. Music has been used for entertainment, rituals and worship. Relatively little is known about the very earliest songs and dances, however, as music from this time would not have been written down. The first people to make use of some form of music notation were the Christian monks in the Medieval period. This means that most of the music that we know of from before the 12th century would have been composed for use in various church services.

PLAINCHANT

This early style of church music is called **plainchant**. It is sometimes referred to as *plainsong* or *Gregorian chant* (named after the 6th century Pope, 'Gregory the Great').

Plainchant consists of a single line melody without any accompanying harmonies or instruments. Plainchant melodies generally move smoothly in small steps rather than wide leaps. They also tend to have quite a limited range of notes, usually within one octave, and would be set to Latin words. The rhythm would be irregular and very free, following the natural rhythms and stresses of the words.

Plainchant melodies were based on types of scales called **modes**. A mode can be found on the piano keyboard, by beginning on any of the white notes and playing up in steps, keeping to the white notes only. A different mode can be found by starting on a different note. Each of the modes has a Greek name. Starting from the note C, the seven different modes are called *Ionian, Dorian, Phrygian, Lydian, Mixolydian, Aeolian* and *Locrian*.

Here is an example of the *Dorian mode*, which can be found by starting on the note D and playing up the white notes in steps to the D an octave higher:

This is the same *Dorian mode*, transposed down one octave into the bass clef:

contd

20

Here is an example of a plainchant melody which makes use of the *Dorian mode*:

Example:

Ky-ri - e————————— e - - le - i-son

Kyrie eleison is a Greek phrase meaning *Lord, have mercy,* and comes from the text of the **Mass**.

Listen to the *Kyrie eleison* while following the printed melody.

As you listen, note the following features of the music:

- the melody is being sung a cappella by a solo male voice
- the music is mainly melismatic (i.e. several notes are sung to one syllable)
- the melody is modal
- the rhythm is very free.

Example:

Here is another example of a plainchant melody which also makes us of the *Dorian mode*:

Vic - ti - mae pa-scha-li lau-des im-mo-lent Chri-sti - a - ni.

A - gnus re - de - mit o - ves: Chri-stus in - no-cens Pa - tri
Mors et vi - ta du - el - o con - fli - xe - re mi - ran - do:

re - con - ci - li - a - vit pec - ca - to - res.
dux vi - tae mor - tu - us, re - gnat vi - vus.

VIDEO LINK

Listen to the tracks featured on this page at www.brightredbooks.net

The Latin phrase *Victimae paschali laudes immolent Christiani* translates roughly as *let Christians offer sacrifice and praise to the passover victim,* and would have been sung on Easter Sunday.

Listen to *Victimae paschali laudes* while following the printed melody.

As you listen, note the following features of the music:

- the melody is being sung a cappella by male voices in unison
- the music is mainly syllabic (i.e. each syllable is sung to a different note)
- the melody is modal
- the rhythm is very free.

DON'T FORGET

Plainchant is a single line melody that is sung unaccompanied.

THINGS TO DO AND THINK ABOUT

Try to find examples of popular songs or traditional tunes that are based on modes.

ONLINE TEST

Test yourself on Sacred music at www.brightredbooks.net/HMusic

MASS

Mass is the most important service in many Christian denominations, including the Roman Catholic and Anglican churches. There are different kinds of Mass, e.g. *Missa Brevis* (a short Mass) or *Requiem* (a Mass for the dead).

SECTIONS OF THE MASS

A typical Mass is divided into five main sections, or *items*. Here are the Latin headings of the five main sections of the Mass, along with English translations:

Latin	English
Kyrie eleison, Christe eleison	Lord have mercy, Christ Have mercy
Gloria in excelcis Deo	Glory to God in the highest
Credo in unum deum	I believe in one God
Sanctus; Osanna; Benedictus	Holy, holy, holy; Hosanna; Blessed is he. . .
Agnus Dei	Lamb of God

The term Mass also refers to a piece of music, generally for a choir, in which the words of the Mass are sung. Many composers throughout history have composed Masses. Not all of these Masses have been intended to be sung as a church service, however. Some have been composed as concert pieces, to be performed in a concert hall.

You will now listen to some contrasting musical settings Masses, by composers from different musical periods and styles.

A MASS FROM THE BAROQUE PERIOD

Example:

Listen to the opening of the *Kyrie eleison* from the *Mass in B minor* by J S Bach while following the printed music.

Notice that there are five voice parts: two soprano parts and one each of alto, tenor and bass.

Johann Sebastian Bach (1685–1750)

contd

As you listen, note the following features of the music:

- the choir is singing in harmony
- the texture is mainly homophonic
- the choir is accompanied by an orchestra
- the tonality of the music is minor
- the fourth bar ends with an imperfect cadence.

Example:

The next example is part of the *Credo* from Bach's *Mass in B minor*.
The music opens with an introduction which is four bars long. The flutes and strings play gentle chords over the following ground bass:

Notice that the ground bass is descending in semitones, using part of a chromatic scale.
After the introduction, the four voices enter one after the other in imitation; soprano, alto, tenor then bass:

VIDEO LINK

Listen to the tracks featured on this page at www.brightredbooks.net

Notice that the ground bass continues throughout.

Listen to whole of the *Crucifixus* from the *Mass in B minor* by J S Bach, following the printed musical examples for the opening.

As you listen, note the following features of the music:

- introduction featuring flutes and strings over a ground bass
- the four voices enter in imitation – soprano, alto, tenor then bass
- the texture in the voices is mainly polyphonic (contrapuntal)
- the ground bass continues throughout the music
- the tonality of the music is minor
- the music ends in the relative major.

DON'T FORGET

A Mass consists of five main sections: *Kyrie, Gloria, Credo, Sanctus* and *Agnus Dei.*

 THINGS TO DO AND THINK ABOUT

Listen to more of the *Kyrie eleison* from Bach's *Mass in B minor*, and consider whether the texture is mainly homophonic or mainly polyphonic.

 ONLINE TEST

Test yourself on Sacred music at www.brightredbooks.net/HMusic

23

A MASS FROM THE CLASSICAL PERIOD

GLORIA FROM THE NELSON MASS BY HAYDN

Listen to opening eight bars of the *Gloria* from the *Nelson Mass* by Haydn while following the printed music.

It begins with a soprano solo for the first two bars. The chorus then repeats these two bars, singing in harmony. The texture here is homophonic, as all the voices are singing exactly the same rhythms. The soprano solo then sings the next four bars, with the chorus joining in for one bar. This opening is quite typical of the Classical style as it is made up from clear-cut regular two-bar phrases.

Franz Joseph Haydn (1732–1809)

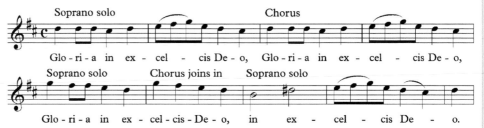

As you listen to this opening, note the following features of the music:

- the music starts with a soprano solo
- the chorus repeats the soprano phrase
- the texture of the chorus is homophonic
- the music is accompanied by an orchestra
- the tonality of the music is major
- this section ends with a perfect cadence.

 ACTIVITY

Listen to the full *Gloria in excelsis Deo* from Haydn's *Nelson Mass* while following the guide to the music in the table below. The Latin text is printed in the left-hand column. The musical features are printed in the right-hand column at the point where they occur in the music. Try to identify the features as you listen to the music.

contd

Gloria in excelsis Deo,	1. Soprano solo.
Gloria in excelsis Deo,	2. SATB choir – homophonic texture.
Gloria in in excelsis Deo, in excelsis Deo.	3. Soprano solo. Choir joining in briefly.
Gloria, in excelsis Deo, Gloria, Gloria, in excelsis, in excelsis Deo.	4. SATB choir – homophonic texture.
Et in terra pax hominibus,	5. Bass and tenor solos in imitation.
pax hominibus,	6. Soprano solo.
Et in terra pax hominibus,	7. Bass and tenor solos in imitation.
bonæ voluntatis.	8. Bass and tenor solos in harmony.
Laudamus te; benedicimus te; adoramus te;	9. Voices in unison.
glorificamus te. Laudamus; benedicimus; adoramus; glorificamus te.	10. Voices in harmony.
Gratias agimus, agimus tibi propter magnam gloriam tuam, propter gloriam tuam.	11. Alto solo.
Domine Deus, Rex coelestis,	12. Soprano solo.
Deus Pater, Deus Pater, Pater omnipotens	13. Sequence.
Domine Fili unigenite, Jesu Christe, Jesu, Jesu Christe.	14. SATB choir – homophonic texture.
Domine Deus, Agnus Dei, Filius Patris.	15. Bass and tenor solos enter in imitation, then sing in harmony.
Domine Deus, Agnus Dei, Filius Patris.	16. Solo voices – homophonic texture.
Domine Deus, Agnus Dei, Filius Patris.	17. SATB choir
Filius Patris.	18. Perfect cadence

Here is a translation of the Latin text:

Glory be to God in the highest.
And in earth peace
to men of good will.

We praise Thee; we bless Thee;
we worship Thee; we glorify Thee.
We give thanks to Thee
for Thy great glory.

O Lord God, Heavenly King,
God the Father Almighty.
O Lord Jesus Christ, the only begotten Son.
Lord God, Lamb of God,
Son of the Father.

 DON'T FORGET

A Mass can be sung either a cappella or with accompaniment.

 VIDEO LINK

Listen to the tracks featured on this page at www.brightredbooks.net

ONLINE TEST

Test yourself on Sacred music at www.brightredbooks.net/HMusic

 THINGS TO DO AND THINK ABOUT

Consider which musical features of Haydn's *Gloria in excelsis Deo* are typical of the Classical style.

MASSES FROM THE ROMANTIC PERIOD AND TWENTIETH CENTURY

Anton Bruckner (1824–1896)

A MASS FROM THE ROMANTIC PERIOD

Bruckner's *Mass No. 3 in F minor* was composed for SATB chorus, soloists and a large orchestra. It is quite typical of music from the Romantic period in that the music is also very expressive, featuring a wide range of dynamics as well as chromatic harmonies.

Example:

Listen to the opening of the *Sanctus* from the *Mass No. 3 in F minor* by Bruckner, while following the printed music.

Here is a guide to the chorus parts of the opening section:

As you listen, note the following features of the music:

- the music starts quietly with woodwind and strings

- the music is slow and has 4 beats in the bar

- the sopranos and altos enter, singing in unison

- the tenors and basses then enter, also singing in unison

- the sopranos and altos alternate with the tenors and basses

- the sopranos and altos start each phrase with the interval of a 4th

- the tenors and basses start each phrase with an octave leap.

As the music continues, listen out for the following:

- SATB chorus sings *Dominus Deus Sabaoth* fortissimo accompanied by chords on the brass, followed by an ascending scale then a descending arpeggio on the strings

- SATB chorus sings *Sanctus* pianissimo followed by soft chords on the woodwind and strings

- SATB chorus sings *Pleni sunt coeli et terra gloria tua* fortissimo accompanied by the full orchestra

- the tempo is faster and the time signature has changed to three beats in the bar

contd

- the soloists and chorus sing *hosanna in excelsis*, alternating as follows:

- the chorus repeats *hosanna in excelsis*, accompanied by the full orchestra

- the music ends fortissimo with prominent dotted rhythms in the brass.

A MASS FROM THE TWENTIETH CENTURY

Listen to opening of the *Agnus Dei* from the *Mass* for four-part choir and wind instruments by Stravinsky while following the printed music.

The music starts with a short introduction played by woodwind and brass, before the choir enters with the following:

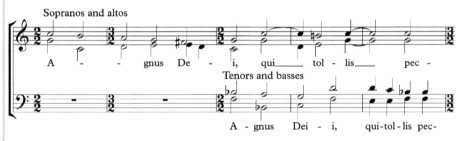

Igor Stravinsky (1882–1971)

As you listen, note the following features of the music:

- introduction played by woodwind and brass

- sopranos and altos start to sing

- tenors and basses join in two bars later

- SATB choir singing a cappella

- the texture is homophonic

- the harmony uses many discords

- there are several time changes (i.e. changes of time signature).

As the music continues, it alternates between sections for SATB choir singing a cappella and sections played by woodwind and brass.

 THINGS TO DO AND THINK ABOUT

Consider which musical features of Stravinky's *Mass* for four-part choir and wind instruments suggest that it was composed in the twentieth century.

 DON'T FORGET

A Mass from any style or period consists of five main sections: *Kyrie, Gloria, Credo, Sanctus* and *Agnus Dei.*

ONLINE TEST

Test yourself on Sacred music at www.brightredbooks.net/ HMusic

 VIDEO LINK

Listen to the tracks featured on this page at www.brightredbooks.net

27

ORATORIO 1

Although sacred music is based on religious words or stories, not all sacred music is composed for church services or religious occasions. Many sacred works have been composed to be performed in concert halls.

ORATORIO

An **oratorio** is a large-scale work for SATB chorus, soloists and orchestra. Oratorios are based on religious stories, often taken from the Bible. Like an opera, an oratorio features recitatives and arias for the soloists, and choruses for the choir to sing. However, whereas an opera would be acted out, with costumes and scenery, an oratorio would be performed with no costumes or scenery. Therefore, while an opera would be staged in an opera house or a theatre, and oratorio would be performed in a church or a concert hall.

An aria is a solo song from an opera or oratorio, usually accompanied by an orchestra.

A **recitative** is a vocal piece where the music follows the natural rhythm of speech. It is used in operas and oratorios to move the story or plot on. A recitative usually leads into an aria or a chorus.

The term chorus can be used to describe either a group of singers, such as a choir, or the music performed by a group of singers. The abbreviation SATB (meaning soprano, alto, tenor, bass) is sometime used to describe a chorus of mixed voices – SATB chorus.

You will now listen to some excerpts from contrasting oratorios, by composers from different musical periods and styles.

An oratorio from the Baroque period

One of the most popular oratorios ever composed is *Messiah* by Handel. *Messiah* is structured in three parts. Part I prophesises the coming of the Messiah and the birth of Christ. Part II tells of the suffering and death of Christ. Part III is about redemption, thanksgiving and resurrection. The music is composed for SATB chorus, four soloists (one each of soprano, alto, tenor and bass), and a Baroque orchestra consisting of strings, woodwind and trumpets.

Example:

Listen to the opening of *For unto us a child is born* from Part I of Handel's *Messiah* while following the printed music.

As you listen, note the following features of the music:

- instrumental introduction
- the music is in the key of G major and has four beats in the bar
- sopranos enter with *For unto us a child is born*
- tenors enter, imitating the opening soprano phrase an octave lower
- sopranos then imitate the tenors
- the soprano singing is melismatic.

contd

Example:

Listen to the recitative *Unto which the angels* and the chorus *Let all the angels* from Part II of Handel's *Messiah*. Examples of the printed music are shown.

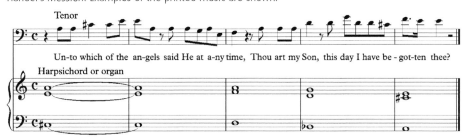

As you listen to the recitative *Unto which the angels*, note the following features of the music:

- the tenor sings the recitative
- the recitative is accompanied by simple chords played on the harpsichord
- the tonality is minor
- the recitative ends with an imperfect cadence.

The chorus *Let all the angels* follows on immediately from the recitative. As you listen to the chorus *Let all the angels*, note the following features of the music:

- the SATB chorus enter, accompanied by the orchestra
- the chorus begins with an anacrusis
- the texture is homophonic
- the tonality is major
- as the music continues the texture becomes polyphonic
- the altos start, immediately followed by the sopranos, then the basses and later the tenors
- the rest of this movement has a polyphonic texture
- the movement finishes with a short instrumental coda
- there is a perfect cadence at the end.

THINGS TO DO AND THINK ABOUT

Look again at the start of the polyphonic section of the chorus *Let all the angels*. The first seven notes in the soprano part (a) are repeated (b) but with the note lengths being half the original value. This shortening of the note values is called **diminution**.

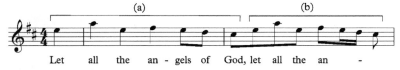

At the very opening of this section the first seven notes of the soprano part (a) are double the value of the first seven notes in the alto part (c). This lengthening of the note values is called **augmentation**.

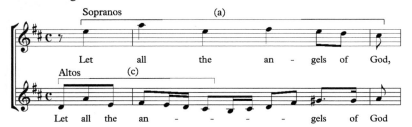

Listen to the chorus *Let all the angels* again and you will notice many further examples of augmentation and diminution.

DON'T FORGET

Augmentation is when the note values of a melody are lengthened.

DON'T FORGET

Diminution is when the note values of a melody are shortened.

ONLINE TEST

Test yourself on Sacred music at www.brightredbooks.net/HMusic

VIDEO LINK

Listen to the tracks featured on this page at www.brightredbooks.net

ORATORIO 2

DON'T FORGET

Oratorios contain recitatives, arias and choruses.

Listen to the recitative *Behold, I tell you a mystery* and the aria *The trumpet shall sound* from Part III of Handel's *Messiah*. Examples of the printed music are shown.

Example:

VIDEO LINK

Listen to the tracks featured on this page at www. brightredbooks.net

As you listen to the recitative *Behold, I tell you a mystery*, note the following features of the music:

- the bass sings the recitative
- the start of the recitative is accompanied by sustained chords on the strings
- the tonality is major
- there is an octave leap on the word 'mystery'
- towards the end of the recitative the strings play short rapid semiquaver – quaver motifs
- the recitative ends with a perfect cadence.

The aria *The trumpet shall sound* follows on immediately from the recitative. During the aria you will hear a solo trumpet providing a prominent and important countermelody. This is called an **obbligato**.

DON'T FORGET

An obligato is a prominent and important instrumental countermelody.

Example:

As you listen to the aria *The trumpet shall sound*, note the following features of the music:

- a long introduction featuring trumpet, strings and harpsichord
- the music has three beats in the bar
- the tonality is major
- the bass solo enters singing 'The trumpet shall sound'
- trumpet and strings play a dotted rhythm
- the bass sings 'and the dead shall be rais'd', and the trumpet continues with a dotted rhythm
- the bass enters again accompanied by a trumpet obbligato.

PLAGAL CADENCE

The *Hallelujah Chorus* from *Messiah* makes us of a chord progression called a **plagal cadence**. This is when chord IV is followed by chord I. For example, in the key of C major this would be the chord of F major followed by the chord of C major. A plagal cadence is sometimes referred to as an 'amen' cadence as it is often used at the end of hymn tunes.

Example:

Listen to the *Hallelujah Chorus* from *Messiah* from Handel's *Messiah*. The last four bars are shown. There are several repeated plagal cadences at the beginning and also towards the end. There is an extended plagal cadence at the very end.

DON'T FORGET

A plagal cadence is a chord progression formed by chords IV-I.

AN ORATORIO FROM THE CLASSICAL PERIOD

The Creation by Haydn was composed for soprano, tenor and bass soloists, SATB chorus and orchestra. *The Creation,* which is in three parts, depicts the creation of the world as described in the *Book of Genesis*. The first part is about the creation of light, heaven and earth, the sun and moon, the land and water, and of plants. The second part is about the creation of the animals, and of man and woman. The third part is about Adam and Eve in the Garden of Eden.

Example:

Listen to opening of *The heavens are telling* from *The Creation* while following the printed music.

Franz Joseph Haydn (1732–1809)

The first part of *The Creation* ends with the mighty chorus *The heavens are telling*. As you listen to this opening, note the following features of the music:

- the music starts with SATB chorus
- the rhythmic feature at the start is an anacrusis
- the texture is homophonic
- the music is accompanied by an orchestra
- the tonality of the music is major
- this phrase ends with an imperfect cadence.

As the music continues, you will notice that is quite typical of the Classical style as it is made up from clear-cut regular four-bar phrases, alternating between the SATB chorus and the strings.

ONLINE

Head to the Digital Zone for an extra activity on this topic.

THINGS TO DO AND THINK ABOUT

Consider the differences between a recitative and an aria, and make sure that you feel confident in recognising either.

Consider which musical features of *The heavens are telling* from *The Creation* are typical of the Classical style.

ONLINE TEST

Test yourself on Sacred music at www.brightredbooks.net/HMusic

ORATORIOS FROM THE ROMANTIC PERIOD AND TWENTIETH CENTURY

Felix Mendelssohn (1809–1847)

AN ORATORIO FROM THE ROMANTIC PERIOD

Mendelssohn's oratorio *Elijah* was composed for soprano, alto, tenor, bass and treble soloists, SATB chorus, boys' chorus, and a large orchestra. It depicts events in the life of the Biblical prophet Elijah, and is in two parts. The first part describes how the prophet brings on a drought in Israel to punish the people for deserting God. The second part tells of Elijah being pursued by his enemies. But, under the protection of the Lord he triumphs over them. *Elijah* is quite typical of music from the Romantic period in that the music is also very expressive, featuring a wide range of dynamics as well as chromatic harmonies.

Example:

Listen to the recitative *Call him louder* followed by the chorus *Hear our cry, O Baal!* The printed music is shown.

DON'T FORGET

A recitative follows the natural rhythm of speech and is used to move the story or plot on. A recitative usually leads into an aria or a chorus.

As you listen to the recitative *Call him louder*, note the following:

- the baritone voice begins the recitative
- this is answered by chords in the woodwind
- the baritone continues, accompanied by sustained chords in the strings
- many of the chords in the strings are chromatic.

As you listen to the chorus *Hear our cry, O Baal!*, note the following:

- the music starts with dramatic repeated notes in the brass
- the SATB chorus enters in imitation: basses, tenors, altos then sopranos

VIDEO LINK

Listen to the tracks featured on this page at www.brightredbooks.net

contd

- the SATB chorus is then homophonic
- the chorus sings a repeat dotted rhythm.

INTERRUPTED CADENCE

The aria *O rest in the Lord* from *Elijah* makes us of a chord progression called an **interrupted cadence**. This is when chord V is followed by chord VI. For example, in the key of C major this would be the chord of G major followed by the chord of A minor. Or, in the key of A minor it would be the chord of E major followed by the chord of C major. An interrupted cadence is sometimes referred to as a 'surprise' cadence as the listener would be expecting chords V–I which would sound more final.

Example:

Listen to *O rest in the Lord* from *Elijah*. This is an aria sung by an alto.

At approximately half way through the aria there are two interrupted cadences.

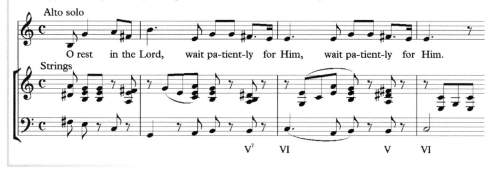

AN ORATORIO FROM THE TWENTIETH CENTURY

Belshazzar's feast by William Walton was composed for baritone solo, chorus and orchestra with a large brass section. Sometimes referred to as a *cantata* (because it is shorter than most oratorios) *Belshazzar's feast* does, nevertheless, contain the musical features that would be associated with an oratorio. The story is based on a scene from the Bible (the *Book of Daniel*). After a feast, Belshazzar, the Babylonian king, insults and outrages the Jews, who are enslaved. Belshazzar is suddenly killed, however, and the Jews regain their freedom.

 THINGS TO DO AND THINK ABOUT

Consider some of the similarities and differences between Handel's *Messiah* and Mendelssohn's *Elijah*.

Consider which musical features of *Belshazzar's feast* suggest that it was composed in the twentieth century.

TIMBRE: INSTRUMENTAL PLAYING TECHNIQUES

TREMOLANDO AND HARMONICS

OVERVIEW

For National 5 Music you will already have learned to identify the sounds of different musical instruments and instrumental groups, as well as a variety of different instrumental playing techniques.

As the Higher Music course builds on previous knowledge and understanding of music concepts at lower levels, you will still be expected to have a secure understanding of the different instruments and instrumental groups introduced at National 3, National 4 and National 5. If you want to revise instruments and instrumental groups from previous levels, you can refer to the Bright Red N5 Music Study Guide.

For Higher Music there are no additional instruments that you will need to be able to recognise. The only additional instrumental group that you may be required to identify is the string quartet, which you can find out more about in the *chamber music* sections of the chapters about *Classical music* and *Romantic music* in this study guide. Remember, however, that you will still be expected to identify any of the individual instruments and instrumental groups from National 3, National 4 or National 5.

For National 5 you will also have learned to identify different instrumental playing techniques such as arco, pizzicato, con sordino and flutter tonguing. For Higher Music there are two additional playing techniques that you will need to be able to recognise: **tremolando** and **harmonics**.

TREMOLANDO

Tremolando is an Italian term that describes either a rapidly repeated note (particularly the rapid up-and-down movement of a bow on a stringed instrument), or the rapid alternation between two different notes at least a 3rd apart.

When a tremolando is used to repeat a single note, it would be notated like this and performed like this .

The use of the tremolando creates an agitated and restless effect.

When a tremolando is used to indicate the rapid alternation between two different notes, it could be notated like this and performed like this.

Be careful not to confuse a tremolando with a trill. A trill is a rapid alternation between two notes a step apart whereas a tremolando is the rapid alternation between to different notes at least a 3rd apart.

contd

Example:

Beethoven, *Piano Sonata No. 8 in C minor, Op. 13*

After a slow introduction, lasting almost two minutes, the much faster *Allegro di molto e con brio* section begins. Notice the tremolando octaves played in the left hand.

 VIDEO LINK

Listen to the first movement of the Piano Sonata No. 8 in C minor, Op. 13 (known as the *Pathétique* Sonata) by Beethoven. Part of the music is shown.

HARMONICS

Harmonics is a term to describe the very high, faint notes (called overtones), produced on a bowed string instrument, or guitar, by lightly touching the strings at certain points.

In music notation harmonics are indicated by a very small circle written above the note to be played.

VIDEO LINK

Listen to the opening of the orchestral piece *In The Steppes of Central Asia* by Borodin at www.brightredbooks.net

Example:

Borodin, *In The Steppes of Central Asia*

Listen to the opening of the orchestral piece *In The Steppes of Central Asia* by Borodin. Part of the music is shown.

VIDEO LINK

Listen to examples of harmonics played on different types of guitars at www.brightredbooks.net.

As you listen, notice the following features in the music:

- the music opens with harmonics played pianissimo on the violins
- the clarinet plays a gentle melody
- the French horn repeats the same melody at a lower pitch
- lower strings then play pizzicato
- a more extended melody is played by the *cor anglais* (a woodwind instrument similar to the oboe but slightly larger)
- the harmonics on the violins continue throughout.

Harmonics can also be played on an acoustic guitar, electric guitar or bass guitar. When played on a guitar, harmonics can sound bell-like.

 **DON'T FORGET**

Harmonics are the very high, faint notes produced on a bowed stringed instrument.

 **THINGS TO DO AND THINK ABOUT**

Consider listening to examples of harmonics being played. You can find some examples for different instruments on the Digital Zone.

 ONLINE TEST

Test yourself on Timbre at www.brightredbooks.net

FORMS, STYLES AND PERIODS

BAROQUE MUSIC 1

The term Baroque is often used to refer to the highly ornamented style of architecture and art fashionable in the 17th century, as well as to the style of music composed around that time.

You will already be familiar with some of the main characteristics of Baroque music as these would have been part of the National 5 Music course. If you want to revise concepts from previous levels, you can refer to the Bright Red N5 Music Study Guide.

CHARACTERISTICS OF BAROQUE MUSIC

Common characteristics of Baroque music include:

- long flowing melodies, often with sequences
- ornaments such as trills and mordents
- contrapuntal (or polyphonic) textures, including the use of imitation.

A trill is a very quick alternation between two notes which are a step apart. In music notation a trill is generally indicated by the abbreviation *tr.* Sometimes this is followed by a wavy line to indicate the length of the trill.

A trill on a short note, such as a crotchet, would be notated like this:

and performed like this:

A trill on a longer note, such as a minim, would be notated with a wavy line like this:

and performed like this:

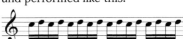

A **mordent** is an ornament which sounds the main note, followed by the note either a step above or below, then the main note again. The two most common types of mordent are shown in music notation below. An upper mordent sounds the main note, the note above, and then the main note again.

An upper mordent would be notated like this:

and performed like this:

A lower mordent sounds the main note, the note below, and then the main note again.

A lower mordent would be notated like this (notice the vertical line through the symbol):

and performed like this:

THE HARPSICHORD

A popular keyboard instrument associated with Baroque music is the harpsichord.

Example:

Listen to the *Two-part invention in C major* by J S Bach played on the harpsichord. The first four bars are printed below.

DON'T FORGET ➕

Ornaments such as trills and mordents are common in Baroque music.

contd

36

Notice the following features in the music:

- the right hand starts playing on its own
- the left hand part imitates the right hand part, an octave lower in the bass clef
- mordents played by the right hand part in the first two bars
- a descending sequence in both the right and left hand parts in the third and fourth bars.

As you listen to more of the piece, notice the contrapuntal (or polyphonic) texture as well as further examples of ornaments, sequences and imitation.

BASSO CONTINUO

As well as playing solo music, the harpsichord was often used to provide an accompaniment for songs and other instrumental pieces. It would have been common practice for the harpsichord player to improvise a chordal accompaniment over a given bass line. This kind of accompaniment is known as a **basso continuo**, sometimes just referred to as **continuo**.

The bass line would generally be played by an instrument such as the cello, double bass or bassoon. The printed music for the bass part would have numbers and music symbols, such as accidentals, printed below the notes. This is known as a *figured bass* and is a form of music notation that would indicate the chords to be played by the harpsichord, much in the same way that keyboard players and guitarists read from printed *guitar chords* today. The harpsichord player would then improvise an appropriate accompaniment using the chords suggested by the *figured bass.*

Here is the opening of the *Sonata in E minor, Opus 5, No. 8* by Arcangelo Corelli, for violin and basso continuo. Notice the solo violin melody on the upper stave, and the bass line on the lower stave with the *figured bass* below the stave.

Here is the same opening, with an example of how the chords might be *realised* on the harpsichord. Notice the solo violin melody is on the upper stave. However, in this example the harpsichord has two staves. The lower stave has the same bass line as before, and this would be played by the performer's left hand. The middle stave has a possible *realisation* of the chords indicated by the *figured bass,* and this would be played by the performer's right hand.

 THINGS TO DO AND THINK ABOUT

Consider the different types of ornaments you might hear in pieces of music (e.g. mordent, acciaccatura and trill). Make sure that you can tell them apart.

 **ACTIVITY**

Listen to the *Sonata in E minor, Opus 5, No. 8* by Arcangelo Corelli played by a solo violin accompanied by a harpsichord, with the harpsichord providing the basso continuo part.

 DON'T FORGET

A mordent is an ornament which comprises the main note, followed by the note either a step above or below, then the main note again.

VIDEO LINK

Listen to an example of a harpsichord playing at www.brightredbooks.net

 **DON'T FORGET.**

The harpsichord is a popular keyboard instrument in Baroque music.

 VIDEO LINK

Find the musical examples for this section on the Digital Zone.

 ONLINE TEST

Test yourself on Baroque music at www.brightredbooks.net

37

BAROQUE MUSIC 2

THE HARPSICHORD

As well as accompanying solo instruments, the harpsichord is often used to provide the accompaniment for songs and musical ensembles.

Here is the opening of the recitative *Thy hand, Belinda*, from the opera *Dido and Aeneas* by *Henry Purcell*. Notice the vocal line on the upper stave, and the basso continuo part on the lower stave with the *figured bass* below the stave.

The harpsichord player would create a chordal accompaniment to the voice, elaborating on the chords indicated by the *figured bass*.

 **ACTIVITY**

Listen to the *Thy hand, Belinda* by Henry Purcell, noting the basso continuo part provided by the harpsichord.

Here is the opening of the *Trio Sonata in D Major, Op. 3, No. 2* by Arcangelo Corelli, for two violins and basso continuo. Notice the 1st violin part on the upper stave, the 2nd violin part on the middle stave, and the basso continuo part on the lower stave with the *figured bass* below the stave. The harpsichord player would play from the basso continuo part and *realise* the *figured bass* by providing a chordal accompaniment.

DON'T FORGET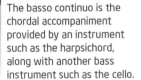

The basso continuo is the chordal accompaniment provided by an instrument such as the harpsichord, along with another bass instrument such as the cello.

ACTIVITY

Listen to the *Trio Sonata in D Major, Op. 3, No. 2* by Arcangelo Corelli for strings and harpsichord. Listen out for the harpsichord playing the basso continuo part.

THE PIPE ORGAN

Another popular keyboard instrument in Baroque music is the pipe organ. In some performance of Baroque music, you may hear an organ providing the basso continuo part instead of a harpsichord.

ACTIVITY

Listen to the *Trio Sonata in D minor, BWV 527* by J S Bach for two violins, cello and organ.

Listen to the *Organ Partita, BWV 768* by J S Bach for recorder, cello and organ.

contd

However, the organ is also a popular solo instrument in Baroque music.

Here is an arrangement of the opening from the *Toccata and Fugue in D minor* by J S Bach:

Example:

DON'T FORGET

A Tierce de Picardie is a major chord at the end of a piece of music in a minor key.

Listen to the opening bars of the *Toccata and Fugue in D minor, BWV 565* by J S Bach for organ.

As you listen, notice the following features in the music:

- the first three phrases, in the first line of the music, all start with a lower mordent
- the second line starts with a pedal note – a long held note in the bass, beneath changing harmonies
- the chord built up over this pedal note is a diminished 7th
- the excerpt ends with a **Tierce de Picardie** – a major chord at the end of a piece of music that's in a minor key.

DON'T FORGET

Find out more about the diminished 7th chord in the Music Literacy section.

PASSACAGLIA

A popular form or structure used in Baroque music is the **passacaglia**. The passacaglia is a set of variations on a ground bass with the following characteristics:

- slow tempo
- triple time (3 beats in a bar)
- based on a short 4 or 8 bar phrase
- often in a minor tonality.

The bass line would be repeated many times, while the upper parts would be varied. While the theme in the bass is repeated unchanged the upper parts become increasingly elaborate.

The *Passacaglia in D minor* by Dieterich Buxtehude is based on the following 4-bar theme:

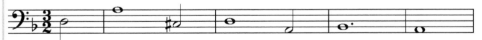

The *Passacaglia in C minor* by J S Bach starts with the following 8-bar theme, played in the bass, which is continuously repeated throughout the music:

DON'T FORGET

A Passacaglia is a repeating bass line, usually with 3 beats in the bar and in a minor key.

VIDEO LINK

Find the musical examples for this section on the Digital Zone.

ONLINE TEST

Test yourself on Baroque music at www.brightredbooks.net

THINGS TO DO AND THINK ABOUT

Listen to the *Passacaglia in D minor* by Dieterich Buxtehude.

Listen to the *Passacaglia in C minor* by J. S. Bach.

In each case, listen out for the repeating passacaglia theme in the bass while the harmonies above become increasingly elaborate.

BAROQUE MUSIC 3

CONCERTO AND CONCERTO GROSSO

Other important instrumental styles and forms associated with Baroque music are the **concerto** and **concerto grosso**. The term concerto, which generally refers to a solo concerto, features a solo instrument accompanied by a string orchestra (called the **ripieno**). The concerto grosso comprises a small group of solo instruments (called the **concertino**) along with the larger ripieno group.

Both types of concerto are often in three movements: quick – slow – quick. The quicker movements are often structured in ritornello form, in which the recurring ritornello theme alternates with themes played by the soloists (called episodes**)**.

Here is the overall plan of **ritornello** form:

Ritornello 1	Episode 1	Ritornello 2	Episode 2	Ritornello 3	and so on. . .
Ripieno	Soloist	Ripieno	Soloist	Ripieno	

The ritornello theme could recur many times, alternating with several different episodes.

It is also common, in both a solo concerto and concerto grosso, to have a continuo part played by a harpsichord, along with a low instrument such as a cello or bassoon. The composer would write a bass line only for the continuo. The harpsichord player would then improvise chords over this bass line to fill out the harmonies.

You should now listen to two different movements; one from a solo concerto and one from a concerto grosso.

The Italian Baroque composer Antonio Vivaldi composed around 500 concertos. A collection of concertos called *The Four Seasons* consists of four solo concertos for violin, string orchestra and continuo. These are descriptive works based on poems describing the four seasons of the year.

Antonio Vivaldi (1678–1741)

ACTIVITY

Listen to the 1st movement of *Spring* from *The Four Seasons* by Vivaldi while following the guide below. Some of the music notation is printed an octave lower than the sounding pitch to make it easier to read.

Ritornello 1

The piece opens with an extended ritornello theme in the bright key of E major. Notice a characteristic Baroque feature of a phrase being played forte (loud) and then repeated piano (soft) creating an *echo* effect.

Joyful Spring is here...

The ritornello theme continues, using some syncopated rhythms. Notice again the characteristic Baroque *echo* effect of the first phrase being played forte (loud) and then repeated piano (soft). There is also a trill on the second last note of each phrase.

contd

Episode 1

The solo violin starts by playing repeated staccato notes with mordents. Two other violins join in, one playing trills and one playing repeated notes. The mordents and trills are used to suggest birdsong.

Birds merrily greet it with their happy songs. . .

Ritornello 2

Only one phrase from second part of the original ritornello theme is heard.

Then we hear a gentler theme using grouped semiquavers.

Streams murmur sweetly, caressed by gentle breezes.

One phrase from the second part of the original ritornello theme is heard in a new key.

Episode 2

The ripieno group plays shuddering tremolandos (rapid repeated notes).

The sky darkens as thunder and lightning announce a strorm.

This alternates with the solo violin playing agitated semiquaver triplets.

 ## THINGS TO DO AND THINK ABOUT

Listen to the 3rd movement of *Autumn* from *The Four Seasons* by Vivaldi. Listen out for the ritornello theme and the episodes in between.

DON'T FORGET

A concerto is a piece of music for a solo instrument with an orchestra.

DON'T FORGET

Ripieno is the term used to describe the string orchestra in a Baroque concerto.

DON'T FORGET

Ritornello is a form in which the recurring theme alternates with themes played by the soloist(s).

ONLINE

Read more on *Spring* on www.brightredbooks.net

ONLINE TEST

Test yourself on Baroque music at www.brightredbooks.net

BAROQUE MUSIC 4

Johann Sebastian Bach
(1685–1750)

CONCERTO GROSSO

The German Baroque composer, Johann Sebastian Bach, composed a great deal of music for both the harpsichord and the organ, as well as many other instrumental and choral pieces.

Between 1708 and 1721 he composed six concertos in the **concerto grosso** form. They became known as the *Brandenburg Concertos* as they were dedicated to a rich nobleman called Christian Ludwig, Margrave of Brandenburg. Each of the six *Brandenburg Concertos* is an example of a concerto grosso. They each feature a ripieno group (strings), a concertino group (soloists), and basso continuo.

In the *Brandenburg Concerto No. 2* the concertino group consists of violin, oboe, recorder (or flute), and trumpet. The trumpet used here is a very high-pitched Baroque trumpet.

Example:

Listen to the 1st movement of the *Brandenburg Concerto No. 2 in F major* by J S Bach.
The movement opens with the both the ripieno and concertino groups playing the following theme together:

Then each of the soloists in the concertino group takes it in turn to play the following contrasting theme, in between occurrences of the opening theme:

The solo instruments from the concertino group take it in turn to play this theme in the following order:

Solo 1: violin, with basso continuo (harpsichord and cello) accompaniment
Solo 2: oboe, with the violin playing the accompaniment
Solo 3: recorder (or flute), with the oboe playing the accompaniment
Solo 4: trumpet, with the recorder (or flute) playing the accompaniment

As the movement continues, listen for further contrasts between the instruments of both ripieno and conertino groups, as well as sequences, ornaments, and the basso continuo.

DON'T FORGET

A concerto grosso is a piece of music for a group of solo instruments (concertino) with a string orchestra (ripieno).

 **ACTIVITY**

Listen to movements from Bach's *Brandenburg Concertos* and try to identify the instruments in the concertino group.

Relative major

The major key which is related to a minor key and shares the same key signature is called the **relative major**. The relative major key can be found by going to the third note of the minor scale. For example, the third note of the A minor scale in C, therefore C major is the relative major of A minor. A piece of music in a minor key will sometime modulate to the relative major, as this is its most closely related major key. It is important that you are able to identify a change from a minor key to the relative major by listening to the music.

DON'T FORGET

Concertino the term used to describe the group of soloists in a Baroque concerto grosso.

 ACTIVITY

Listen to *Menuet in A minor* by Krieger while following the melody. The music is in ternary (ABA) form. Section A is in the key of A minor. Section B in the key of C major – the relative major. Section A2 returns to the tonic key of A minor.

contd

As you listen, notice the following features in the music:

Example:

Section A

Section A:

- the music is in the key of A minor
- there are three beats in every bar
- there is a trill towards the end of the section
- the section ends with a perfect cadence in the key of A minor
- the music is repeated with ornaments added.

VIDEO LINK

Head to www.brightredbooks.net to listen to the tracks for this section.

Example:

Section B

Section B:

- the music is in the key of C major – the relative major key
- there is a sequence
- there is a trill towards the end of the section
- the music ends with a perfect cadence in the key of C major.

Example:

Section A2

ONLINE TEST

Test yourself on Baroque music at www.brightredbooks.net

Section A2:

- the music returns to the key of A minor
- the melody from section A is repeated
- there is a trill towards the end of the section
- the section ends with a perfect cadence in the key of A minor.

Sections B and A are then repeated with ornaments added.

THINGS TO DO AND THINK ABOUT

Listen to other examples of music which starts in a minor key and modulates to the relative major. In each case listen carefully for the change between the minor key and the relative major.

VIDEO LINK

Head to www.brightredbooks. net to listen to the pieces mentioned in this topic!

1. *Rondeau* from *Abdelazer* by Purcell.

The music is in rondo (ABACA) form. The main rondo theme is in a minor key. However, the first episode (contrasting section) is in the relative major key.

2. *Impertinence* by Handel.

The music is in binary (AB) form. Section A is in a minor key. Section B starts in the relative major key and then returns to the minor key.

CLASSICAL MUSIC 1

Many of the concepts associated with Classical music were covered at National 5 level. If you want to revise concepts from previous levels, you can refer to the Bright Red N5 Music Study Guide.

INTRODUCTION

For Higher Music, the additional concepts that you will need to be familiar with include **Sonata, Chamber music, String quartet** and **Sonata form**. Common characteristics of Classical music include:

Wolfgang Amadeus
Mozart (1756–1791)

- clear-cut evenly balanced phrases, often two, four or eight bars long
- graceful melodies, often using the notes of the key-chord or scale
- repetition of melodies
- ornaments such as the trill or and acciaccatura
- accompaniments based on broken chord patterns such as the Alberti bass.

SONATA

A **Sonata** is a piece of music for one or two instruments, usually in three or four movements. Sonatas were often composed either for solo piano or another instrument with piano accompaniment. The different movements of a **sonata** would be contrasted by tempo, key and mood, and generally followed the same basic plan:

1. a fairly fast tempo – **allegro** (structured in **sonata form**)

2. a slow tempo – **andante** or **adagio** – more lyrical and song-like (often in **ternary form (ABA)** or **theme and variations**)

3. sometimes a minuet and trio (a dance with three beats in the bar) or possibly the much faster scherzo

4. a fast tempo – **allegro** (commonly structured in **rondo form, sonata form**, or a mixture of the two).

Example:

Listen to the opening of the 2nd movement from Sonata in C K.545 by Mozart, while following the printed music.

As you listen, notice the following features in the music:

- the music is in the key of G major
- there are three beats in every bar
- the tempo is Andante – a slow walking speed
- the left hand features an Alberti bass
- the graceful melody is mainly in cleat-cut two-bar phrases.

Sonata form

Sonata form is the form used in the first movements of sonatas, symphonies, concertos and string quartets. A movement structured in sonata form has three main section, called exposition, *development* and *recapitulation*. Some movements in sonata form also have a slow introduction at the beginning and a coda at the end.

In the *exposition* section the composer introduces two musical themes, called the *first subject* and the *second subject*. A *subject* is a musical theme, or a group of musical ideas.

DON'T FORGET

An Alberti bass is a type of broken chord accompaniment played in the left hand of the piano.

ONLINE

Visit www.brightredbooks.net to listen to the pieces mentioned on these pages and to find additional activities, videos, tests and more.

DON'T FORGET

A piece of music in sonata form has three main section – *exposition, development* and *recapitulation.*

contd

The *first subject* would appear in the tonic key. This would be followed by a *bridge passage* which modulates to a new key. The *second subject* would then appear in a related key. If the music starts in a major key, it would usually modulate to the dominant key. If the music starts in a minor key, it would usually modulate to the relative major.

In the *development* section, the composer may explore and develop melodic, harmonic or rhythmic ideas presented in the *exposition*, or introduce new musical ideas.

The *recapitulation* repeats the music from the *exposition* section with some slight differences. The *first subject* returns in the tonic key. However, the *bridge passage* is now altered so that the *second subject* also returns in the tonic key.

See the basic plan of **sonata form** below.

Exposition	Development	Recapitulation
First subject (tonic key)	Developing ideas from the Exposition.	**First subject** (tonic key)
Bridge (modulating to a new key)	Adding new ideas. Exploring new keys.	**Bridge** (altered)
Second subject (related key)		**Second subject** (tonic key)

Example:

Listen to the first movement of the Sonatina in C, Op. 36, No. 1 by Clementi while following the melody. This movement from a Sonatina ('little sonata'), features the important characteristics of sonata form on a small scale.

As you listen, notice the following features in the music:

Exposition (bars 1–15)

- the first subject (bars 1–4) is in the tonic key of C major
- bars 1–2 outline the tonic chord of C major
- bars 3–4 are based on the scale of C major
- bars 5–8 form the bridge passage
- bars 5–6 are almost the same as bars 1–2
- in bars 7–8 the F sharps suggest a modulation to the key of G major
- the second subject (bars 9–15) is in the dominant key of G major
- a melodic feature of the second subject is the use of octave leaps (bars 9 and 11)
- a repeat sign at the end of bar 15 indicates that the *Exposition* section should be repeated.

Development (bars 16–23)

- bars 16–19 are based on melodic ideas from the first subject but now in a minor key
- bars 20–21 are based on the octave leap idea from the second subject but now developed into an inverted pedal
- bars 22–23 are based on a melodic idea from the first subject.

Recapitulation (bars 24–38)

- repeat of the first subject (bars 24–27) is in the tonic key of C major, an octave lower than before
- bars 28–31 repeat the bridge passage, which is now altered as it does not modulate
- repeat of the second subject (bars 32–35) now remaining in the tonic key of C major

- an end repeat sign at the end of bar 38 and a start repeat sign at the beginning of bar 16 indicates that the *Development* and *Recapitulation* sections should be repeated.

 THINGS TO DO AND THINK ABOUT

Listen to the examples of music in sonata form on the Digital Zone, and try to identify the first and second subjects in the exposition.

CLASSICAL MUSIC 2

Painting of musicians performing chamber music, by Adolph Menzel (1850–52)

CHAMBER MUSIC

Chamber music is music composed for a small group of performers. It is generally intended to be performed in a palace chamber or large room rather than a large concert hall.

Chamber music groups would generally take their name from the number of performers in the group, for example; trio (three performers), quartet (four performers), quintet (five performers), sextet (six performers), septet (seven performers) and octet (eight performers). One of the most popular forms of chamber music is the **string quartet**.

STRING QUARTET

A **string quartet** is music composed for a very specific group of four performers: two violins, a viola and a cello.

The term *string quartet* can be used in two ways. As well as being used to describe the group of performers that make up a string quartet, it can also be used to describe the piece of music composed for a string quartet.

A painting by Julius Schmid, of Franz Joseph Haydn (1732–1809) playing in one of his own string quartets.

ACTIVITY

Listen to the first movement of String Quartet Op. 64 No. 5 ('*The Lark*') by Haydn.

The music is in sonata form. Here is a brief outline of the exposition section.

The first subject starts with a short phrase played staccato by the second violin and viola, answered by an ascending arpeggio phrase on the cello. The second violin and viola continue with a rising sequence followed by a falling sequence, while the cello provides a bass line.

Example:

The first violin then enters with a soaring melody (shown an octave lower than the sounding pitch), which is what gave this quartet the nickname 'The Lark'. The melody features acciaccaturas (grace notes) and trills.

contd

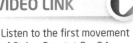

VIDEO LINK

Listen to the first movement of String Quartet Op. 64 No. 5 by Haydn at www.brightredbooks.net

46

Example:

The first violin continues with a descending sequence, dotted rhythms and acciaccaturas (shown an octave lower than the sounding pitch).

Example:

Following a legato phrase with chromatic notes the bridge passage modulates to the dominant key.

The second subject starts, using a syncopated rhythm (shown an octave lower than the sounding pitch).

Example:

The second subject continues, with triplet quavers played by the first violin.

Example:

The exposition ends with a short coda, which refers back to musical ideas from the first subject.

THINGS TO DO AND THINK ABOUT

Listen to the second movement of String Quartet Op. 76 No. 3 ('*The Emperor*') by Haydn.

The movement is in theme and variations form, and is based on a melody that Haydn composed as a national anthem for Austria.

VIDEO LINK

Listen to the *The Emperor String Quartet* by Haydn on www.brightredbooks.net

There are four variations, with each of the instruments of the string quartet being given an opportunity to play the melody.

Variation 1 is a duet for the two violins. The second violin plays the melody, while the first violin provides an accompaniment.

Variation 2 features the cello playing the melody. The second violin and viola provide an accompaniment while the first violin play a high intricate countermelody.

Variation 3 features the viola playing the melody. The first and second violins provide a syncopated accompaniment. The cello then enters with a chromatic bass line.

Variation 4 features the first violin playing the melody but with different harmonies. The movement ends with a short coda which makes use of discords and a tonic pedal.

ONLINE TEST

Test yourself on Classical music at www.brightredbooks.net

ROMANTIC MUSIC

Romantic music tends to be very expressive and was often influenced by historical events, political issues, art, literature or nature. As well as developments in large forms such as the symphony, concerto and opera, the Romantic style also encompassed characterful piano pieces, lieder, song-cycles and chamber music.

Common characteristics of Romantic music include extended melodies, chromatic harmonies, greater freedom in form, unexpected modulations, a wide range of dynamics, and the use of rubato.

Frédéric Chopin (1810–1849)

ROMANTIC PIANO MUSIC

Several improvements were made to the piano during the 19th century. The range of notes increased and the piano gained a richer sound and a wider dynamic range. As well as sonatas and concertos, many short piano pieces were composed which had descriptive titles intended to convey a particular mood or character. Other kinds of music composed for the piano included dances (with titles like *waltz*, *mazurka* and *polonaise*) and shorter expressive pieces (with titles such as *rhapsody*, *romance*, *ballade* and *nocturne*).

Example:

Listen to the first section of the Waltz in A Flat, Op. 69 No. 1 for piano by Chopin. The music for the opening is shown.

As you listen, notice the following features in the music:

- the music is in a major key
- there are three beats in every bar
- the music starts with an anacrusis (an upbeat)
- there are acciaccaturas (grace notes) at the start of the second and third lines
- a number of accidentals (flats, sharps and naturals) shows that the music is very chromatic
- chromatic notes appear in the melody, harmony and the bass line
- the rhythm features a number of triplets
- the music contains a number of dynamic markings such as p (piano), f (forte) and crescendo and diminuendo signs
- there is a *rit.* at the end and the overall tempo has a feeling of rubato.

ONLINE

Head to www.brightredbooks.net for videos, activities, tests and more.

DON'T FORGET

Rubato is an Italian term describing a performer changing the tempo of a piece of music slightly, to make it sound more expressive.

ROMANTIC CHAMBER MUSIC

Chamber music continued to flourish in the Romantic period, with many composers writing music for string quartet.

Example:

Listen to the first section of *Nocturne* from String Quartet No. 2 by Borodin. The opening melody is printed.

A String Quartet

As you listen, notice the following features in the music:

- the music is in a major key
- there are three beats in every bar
- the cello plays an expressive melody, accompanied by the two violins and viola
- the melody features mordents
- the rhythm features triplets
- the two violins and viola are playing a syncopated rhythm in the accompaniment
- the cello repeats the opening melody
- the two violins and viola continue to play a syncopated rhythm in the accompaniment
- the first violin then plays the same expressive melody
- the viola accompanies the violin playing legato quavers
- the second violin and cello are playing long notes
- the cello plays a pedal note and then starts to descend by semitones.

Romantic orchestral music

The orchestra expanded in the Romantic period, with the addition of more instruments in all four sections:

- the string section increased in numbers and the harp became part of the orchestra
- brass instruments became more versatile because of the development of valves and the tuba became part of the brass section
- the woodwind section now included the piccolo, *cor anglais* (a larger version of the oboe), *contrabassoon* (a larger version of the bassoon) and *bass clarinet* (a larger version of the clarinet), and composers sometimes wrote for woodwind instruments in threes or fours
- the percussion section increased with more timpani and a wider range of instruments such as the snare drum, bass drum, cymbals, triangle, tambourine, glockenspiel, xylophone and tubular bells.

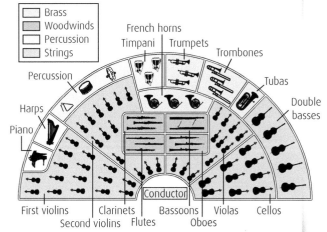

Composers could now use a wider range of timbre (instrumental sounds and playing techniques) and dynamics to compose very expressive and dramatic orchestral works.

 THINGS TO DO AND THINK ABOUT

Listen to some examples of piano music, chamber music, symphonies and concertos by different composers. Consider which particular features of the melody, harmony, rhythm, tempo, timbre and dynamic contribute to making the music sound either Classical or Romantic.

⊕ DON'T FORGET

Chamber music is music composed for a small group of performers.

⊕ DON'T FORGET

A string quartet consists of two violins, a viola and a cello.

⊕ DON'T FORGET

The first movement of any symphony, string quartet, concerto or sonata is always in sonata form.

⊙ VIDEO LINK

Listen to the beginning of the first movement from symphony No. 9 *From the New World*, by Dvořák at www.brightredbooks.net

TWENTIETH CENTURY MUSIC

IMPRESSIONIST MUSIC

A wide range of musical styles emerged during the twentieth century. While some composers adopted quite a traditional approach to music, others took a very experimental approach.

You will already be familiar with some concepts associated with twentieth-century music (including whole-tone scale, atonal, cluster and Minimalist) as these would have been part of the National 5 Music course. If you want to revise concepts from previous levels, you can refer to the Bright Red N5 Music Study Guide.

For Higher Music, the two twentieth-century styles that you will need to be familiar with are **Impressionist** music and **Musique concrète**

Houses of Parliament (1903) by Monet

IMPRESSIONIST MUSIC

Impressionist music was a style of music that developed in the early part of the twentieth century. The term Impressionist was borrowed from a style of painting in which the images were often blurred and hazy. Rather than trying to make their paintings look *real*, as in a photograph, the Impressionist artists wanted to give an *impression* of what the eye might take in at a single glance.

Early twentieth-century Impressionist composers, such as Claude Debussy and Maurice Ravel, attempted to incorporate the same vague, hazy feelings into their music. Common characteristics of Impressionist music include:

- the use of descriptive titles
- discords and chromatic harmonies, often providing a *blurry* effect
- the use of modes, pentatonic scales and whole-tone scales
- fluid rhythms, a vague sense of pulse and a lot of rubato
- a wide variety of instrumental sounds and playing techniques in orchestral music.

Whole-tone scale

A common feature of Impressionist music is the use of the whole-tone scale.

The whole-tone scale is made up from notes that are a tone apart:

Here are the notes of the whole-tone scale, starting on middle C:

C   D   E   F#   G#   A#   (C)

If you look at a keyboard you will notice that the whole-tone scale gets its name from the fact that it contains only tones and avoids the use of semitones.

Claude Debussy (1862–1918)

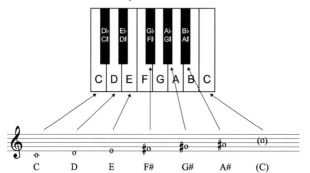

C   D   E   F#   G#   A#   (C)

50

contd

Voiles is example of Impressionist music for solo piano by Debussy. The title can be translated into English as either *veils* or *sails*. The music is very atmospheric and, although it is clearly written with a time signature indicating two beats in the bar, the sense of pulse is very vague.

Example:

Listen to *Voiles* by Debussy. The opening of the music is shown.

As you listen, notice the following features in the music:

- the right hands starts quietly, playing a descending phrase in 3rds

- the opening phrase outline part of a whole-tone scale

- this is immediately followed by an octave leap

- the opening phrase repeats, but now develops into a descending whole-tone scale

- the left hand then plays a repeated low note

- the right hand enters with a short ascending phrase using whole-tones

- the left hand continues to repeat the same low note which has now become a pedal note, and is repeated throughout the entire piece

- the music continues with melodic fragments and harmonies based mainly on the whole-tone scale, although the pentatonic scale is also used briefly.

Reflets dans l'eau (*Reflections in the Water*) by Debussy is another typical example of Impressionist music for solo piano. It is intended to create a musical *impression* of water being not quite still, flowing rapidly, and then slowing down again.

Bridge over a Pond of Water Lilies (1899) by Monet

 **ACTIVITY**

Listen to *Reflets dans l'eau* (*Reflections in the Water*) by Debussy.

As you listen to the music, notice the use of rippling arpeggios and broken chord patterns. The sense of pulse is very vague and the music is played using a lot of rubato. The music also makes use of the pentatonic scale, the whole-tone scale and chromatic harmonies.

THINGS TO DO AND THINK ABOUT

Listen to parts of *La Mer* (*The Sea*) by Debussy. *La Mer* is a series of three *Symphonic Sketches* with individual titles:

- *From dawn to midday on the Sea*

- *Play of the waves*

- *Dialogue of the wind and the Sea*

As you listen to parts of the individual movements, consider which features of the music evoke, or creates an *impression* of, different aspects of the sea. Try to identify features under the headings melody, harmony, rhythm, tempo, timbre and dynamics.

 **DON'T FORGET**

Common features of Impressionist music include the use of whole-tone scales, discords, chromatic harmonies and a vague sense of pulse.

 ONLINE

Head to the Digital Zone for an additional activity on Debussy's *Prélude à l'après-midi d'un faune* and to listen to the pieces mentioned in this topic.

 ONLINE TEST

Test yourself on Twentieth-century music at www.brightredbooks.net

MUSIQUE CONCRÈTE

Pierre Schaeffer (1910–1995)

USING RECORDED SOUNDS

Musique concrète is a style of music that makes use of recorded sounds. The sounds can be natural, such as birds singing or water running. Or, the sounds could be deliberately created, such as a door slamming, a clock ticking or the noises made by traffic or machinery. The recorded sounds are then modified using simple editing techniques such as cutting and re-assembling, playing backwards, slowing down or speeding up. Some composers have combined Musique concrète techniques with electronic sounds or acoustic instruments.

Pierre Schaeffer

The French composer Pierre Schaeffer composed a collection of pieces in 1948 called *Cinq études de bruits* (*Five Studies of Noises*). These five études (studies) were the earliest pieces of Musique concrète. The first étude, *Étude aux chemins de fer* (*Study for railways*) features recordings of sounds made by trains running along the railway tracks.

VIDEO LINK

Listen to the tracks for the activities on this page at www.brightredbooks.net

ACTIVITY

Listen to *Étude aux chemins de fer* (*Study for railways*) by Pierre Schaeffer. As you listen, notice the following features:

- the piece is divided into sections, indicated by the sound of a train whistle
- some of the sounds are repeated, in a *loop*, creating an ostinato effect
- some of the recorded sounds slow down to half-speed causing them to sound distorted
- the piece starts and finishes with the sound of a train whistle.

Karlheinz Stockhausen

The German composer Karlheinz Stockhausen experimented with combining natural sounds with electronic sounds and conventional instruments. In one of his most famous pieces, *Kontakte*, Stockhausen brings together sounds recorded on tape with live instruments. Stockhausen's aim was to try and make 'contact' between:

- pitched notes and noises
- instrumental sounds and electronic sounds
- live performance and pre-recorded sounds.

Karlheinz Stockhausen (1928–2007)

Score for *Kontakte* by Stockhausen

contd

The score for *Kontakte* uses a variety of signs and symbols created by Stockhausen, along with some aspects of conventional musical notation. The upper section of the score uses symbols to indicate electronic sounds on pre-recorded tape along with recorded fragments of vocal sounds. The middle section is for percussion instruments that would be played live. The lower section of the score is for piano and also percussion instruments, that would be played live by the same performer.

ACTIVITY

Listen to part of *Kontakte* by Stockhausen. As you listen, notice the following features:

- electronic sounds changing and transforming
- some of the sounds are similar to helicopter blades speeding up and slowing down
- some of the sounds are similar to a car motor trying to start
- pre-recorded vocal sounds using vowels and consonants
- piano sounds
- percussion sounds
- electronic sounds resembling piano and percussion sounds.

MUSIQUE CONCRÈTE IN POPULAR MUSIC

Musique concrète techniques have also been used by musicians and record producers in different styles of popular music.

The Beatles

The Beatles experimented with a number of different techniques and effects including multi-track recording, overdubbing, tape loops, and electronic manipulation of sounds.

ACTIVITY

Listen to *Tomorrow Never Knows* from the album *Revolver* by The Beatles. The song contains many different influences. As you listen, notice the following features:

- prominent drum kit
- drum sound altered using recording techniques including 'reverse cymbals'
- influence of Indian music through the use of a drone and sitar
- bass guitar riff
- the recording includes natural sounds such as laughing
- the recording of laughing is played at double speed to produce a 'seagull' sound
- the vocal melody is modal
- the electric guitar solo is distorted using recording techniques including being played in reverse
- the structure of the song is strophic (i.e. each verse has the same music).

Other songs that use Musique concrète techniques include *Revolution 9*, from the *White Album* by The Beatles and *Money*, from the album *Dark Side of The Moon*, by Pink Floyd.

THINGS TO DO AND THINK ABOUT

Think about how you might incorporate some Musique concrète techniques into a composition of your own. Consider what sounds you might wish to use, how you might record the sounds, and how you might modify or manipulate the sounds.

DON'T FORGET

Musique concrète makes use of recorded sounds which are then edited and manipulated using recording techniques.

The Beatles

ONLINE

Find an additional activity on *Revolution 9* by the Beatles on the Digital Zone.

ONLINE TEST

Test yourself on Twentieth century music at www.brightredbooks.net

MUSIC LITERACY

CONCEPTS AND MELODY/HARMONY

Music literacy is about understanding music notation. You will have opportunities to explore many of the music literacy concepts through performing music, listening to music and creating your own music. However, there are a number of music literacy concepts that you will need to know for the Higher Music question paper.

ONLINE TEST

Test yourself on
Music Literacy at
www.brightredbook.com

DON'T FORGET

For the Higher Music course
you will also need to know
the music concepts from
National 3, National 4 and
National 5.

CONCEPTS

The music literacy concepts for Higher Music build on previous knowledge and understanding of music concepts at lower levels. You will be expected to have a secure understanding of the music literacy concepts at National 3, National 4 and National 5 levels, in addition to knowledge and understanding of the Higher Music literacy concepts. If you want to revise concepts from previous levels, you can refer to the Bright Red N5 Music Study Guide.

This table lists all the music literacy concepts that are introduced at Higher level.

Melody/harmony	Rhythm/tempo	Texture/ structure/form	Dynamics/ timbre
Bass clef: E – C (range of notes from E below the stave to middle C)	Quavers, crotchets, dotted crotchets and dotted minims within	Phrase mark	Accents (>) Slurs Staccato (.)
Transposing from treble clef down one octave into bass clef	6 9 12		
Identifying chords I, IV, V and VI in major and minor keys in treble and bass clefs	8 8 8 time Triplet quavers, triplet crotchets		
Identifying tonic, subdominant and dominant notes in the keys of C, G and F major and A minor	Rests – quaver, crotchet, dotted crotchet, minim, semibreve, whole bar		
Naming diatonic intervals: 2nd, 3rd, 4th, 5th, 6th, 7th and octave	Da capo (D.C.)		
Writing diatonic intervals above a given note in treble clef			

Music Literacy Concepts for Higher Music

This section provides an overview of all the music literacy concepts introduced at Higher, under the headings **Melody/harmony, Rhythm/tempo, Texture/structure/form** and **Dynamics/timbre**.

MELODY/HARMONY

In music notation, notes are written on five lines and four spaces called a stave or a staff.

For most melody instruments there will a sign called a treble clef at the beginning of the stave. Bass instruments; such as the trombone, cello, double bass and bass guitar, as well as the left hand part of the piano; also make use of the bass clef. For Higher Music, you will need to be familiar with the notes on both the treble clef and bass clef.

Treble clef

Notes on the treble clef stave

From the music literacy concepts at National 4 you should already be aware of a wide range of notes on the treble clef.

Lines and spaces of the treble clef

The treble clef indicates that the lines and spaces have particular names, named after the first seven letters of the alphabet.

contd

The five lines of the treble clef are:

E   G   B   D   F

The four spaces of the treble clef are:

F   A   C   E

Treble clef stave C–A

The notes that you should already know on the treble clef ranges from middle C (on the ledger line below the stave) to high A (on the ledger line above the stave):

C D E F G A B C D E F G A

Bass clef

Lines and spaces of the bass clef

The bass clef sign indicates that the lines and spaces have particular letter names which are different from the treble clef. The lines and spaces on the bass clef are still named after the first seven letters of the alphabet, but are lower in pitch than the treble clef.

The five lines of the bass clef are:

G   B   D   F   A

The four spaces of the bass clef are:

A   C   E   G

Bass clef stave E–C

The notes that you will also need to know on the bass clef range from low E (on the ledger line below the stave) to middle C (on the ledger line above the stave):

E F G A B C D E F G A B C

Transposing down on octave from treble clef to bass clef

One of the music literacy requirements in the Higher Music question paper is to transpose notes down one octave from the treble clef into the bass clef.

Here is the scale of C major, in the treble clef, starting on middle C:

C   D   E   F   G   A   B   C

Here is the scale of C major, transposed down one octave into the bass clef, starting on the C an octave below middle C.

C   D   E   F   G   A   B   C

Here are examples of phrases from melodies, written in the treble clef, and transposed down an octave into the bass clef, that illustrate some points to be aware of.

Here is the opening *Hungarian Dance No. 5* by Brahms, in the key of A minor. Notice the G sharp accidental in the third bar.

Here is the same melody transposed down one octave into the bass clef. Remember to include any accidentals when transposing into the bass clef.

Here is the opening of *Largo* by Handel, in the key of F major. Notice the tied note from the first to the second bar, the dotted rhythm in the second bar, and the triplets in the fourth bar.

Here is the same melody transposed down one octave into the bass clef. Remember to include any ties, dotted notes or triplets when transposing notes down an octave into the bass clef.

These examples are quite long and are given simply to illustrate some melodic and rhythmic issues that you might encounter when transposing notes down one octave from the treble clef into the bass clef. In the Higher Music question paper, however, you will only be required to transpose a small number of notes, probably no more than a bar or so. Part of a blank bass clef stave will be provided for you to do this. The following example is more typical in terms of the number of notes that you are likely to be asked to transpose.

Here is a short phrase, from *Caprice* by Paganini, which makes use of dotted crotchets and quavers, as well as a B flat accidental.

Here is the same phrase transposed down one octave into the bass clef. Remember to include any accidentals when transposing into the bass clef, and write them clearly before the note. Also, make sure to write any dots very clearly immediately after the appropriate note.

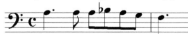

INTERVALS

NAMING AN INTERVAL

For National 5 Music you were required to identify the difference between a tone and a semitone. For Higher Music you will be required to name an interval formed between two notes. When naming an interval formed between two notes, always count from the lower note to the higher note. Count the lower note as 1, and then count up in steps until you reach the number of the upper note. The only intervals you will be required to identify will be a **2nd, 3rd, 4th, 5th, 6th, 7th** or **octave**.

ONLINE

Visit the Digital Zone for tests, activities and more.

EXAMPLES OF INTERVALS

Here are examples of all the intervals in the key of F major, with each interval being shown above tonic note (F):

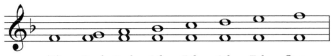

(1)   2nd 3rd   4th   5th   6th   7th   Octave

Here are examples of all the intervals in the key of G major, with each interval being shown below tonic note (G):

Octave 7th   6th   5th   4th   3rd   2nd   (1)

Remember to count from the lower note to the higher note.

If two notes are played together this is known as a harmonic interval.

In this case you count from the lower note up to the higher note, which would be a 5th (C–G).

If the two notes are played one after the other, this is known as a melodic interval.

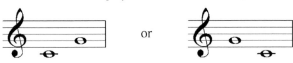

or

The interval is still a 5th, however, as when you count from the lower note to the higher note the lower note is still C and the higher note is still G.

DIATONIC INTERVALS

In the Higher Music question paper, you may be asked to write a diatonic interval (i.e. a note in a particular scale) above a given note in the treble clef. Always remember to count the lower note as 1, and then count up in steps until you reach the number of the upper note.

In other cases, however, you may be asked to name an interval in a melodic context.

contd

Example:

Here are examples of different melodic intervals in different keys.

Melodic intervals in the key of C major.

| 3rd | 4th | Octave | 7th | 5th | 6th | 2nd |

Melodic intervals in the key of G major.

| 2nd | 7th | 3rd | 6th | Octave | 4th | 5th |

Melodic intervals in the key of F major.

| 4th | 6th | 2nd | 5th | 3rd | 7th | Octave |

In the Higher Music question paper, however, you would be expected to name the interval formed by any two notes within a melody. The notes would have a box round them, and you would be required to write the answer in the appropriate place in the box. In the *Things to do and think about* there are some examples of how this might look.

 ## THINGS TO DO AND THINK ABOUT

In this example the lower note is C and the upper note is F. Counting up from C, remembering to count C as 1, the note F is four notes above C. The answer, therefore would be a 4th.

In this example the lower note is C and the upper note is E. Counting up from C, remembering to count C as 1, the note E is three notes above C. The answer, therefore would be a 3rd.

In this example the lower note is G and the upper note is E. Counting up from G, remembering to count G as 1, the note E is six notes above G. The answer, therefore would be a 6th.

 **DON'T FORGET**

Remember to count an interval from the lower note to the higher note.

 **ONLINE TEST**

Test yourself on Intervals at www.brightredbooks.net

HARMONIC AND MELODIC MINOR SCALES

KEY SIGNATURES

For National 5 Music, you will already have learned about the scales and key signatures of C major, G major, F major and A minor. If you would like to revise these scales and key signatures, you can refer to the Bright Red N5 Music Study Guide.

For Higher Music, you will need to be able to distinguish between the two different kinds of minor scales: the **harmonic minor scale** and the **melodic minor scale**. The harmonic minor scale, like the major scale, is exactly the same both ascending and descending. The melodic minor scale, however, is not the same ascending and descending. In the ascending form of the melodic minor scale the 6th and 7th notes are raised by a semitone. In the descending form of the melodic minor scale the raised 6th and 7th notes would be lowered. To illustrate the differences between the harmonic and melodic minor scales, here is the scale of A minor in both forms with the number of the notes (known as the degree of the scale) shown underneath.

In the ascending form of the harmonic minor scale the 7th note (or 7th degree of the scale) is raised by a semitone. In the case of A harmonic minor the 7th note (G) is raised to a G sharp.

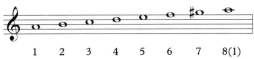

In the descending form of the harmonic minor scale the 7th note (or 7th degree of the scale) is still raised by a semitone. In the case of A harmonic minor the 7th note (G) is still raised to a G sharp.

In the ascending form of the melodic minor scale both the 6th and 7th notes (or 6th and 7th degrees of the scale) are each raised by a semitone. In the case of A melodic minor, the 6th note (F) is raised to an F sharp and the 7th note (G) is raised to a G sharp.

In the descending form of the melodic minor scale, both the 6th and 7th notes (or 6th and 7th degrees of the scale) would not be raised. In the case of A melodic minor, the 6th note (F) would remain as F natural and the 7th (G) would remain as G natural.

TONIC, SUBDOMINANT AND DOMINANT NOTES

In all scales, the different notes (or degrees of the scale) are known by technical terms as well as numbers. For Higher Music you will be expected to know three of these:

- **Tonic** – the first note (or first degree) of the scale
- **Subdominant** – the fourth note (or fourth degree) of the scale
- **Dominant** – the fifth note (or fifth degree) of the scale

In the Higher Music question paper, you could be asked identify the tonic, subdominant or dominant notes in the keys of C major, G major, F major and A minor.

Key	Tonic	Subdominant	Dominant
C major	C	F	G
G major	G	C	D
F major	F	Bb	C
A minor	A	D	E

The table shows these notes, in both treble and bass clefs, in the keys of C major, G major, F major and A minor. In most cases the notes are shown in both the upper and lower octave. Where a note is not shown in both octaves, this is because the other octave is outwith the range of note you would be expected to identify for Higher Music.

DON'T FORGET

You could be expected to recognise either a harmonic or melodic minor scale by hearing an example in an excerpt of music.

contd

Key	Treble clef	Bass clef
C major	(notation) 1 Tonic, 4 Subdominant, 5 Dominant	(notation) 1 Tonic, 4 Subdominant, 5 Dominant
G major	(notation) 1 Tonic, 4 Subdominant, 5 Dominant	(notation) 1 Tonic, 4 Subdominant, 5 Dominant
F major	(notation) 1 Tonic, 4 Subdominant, 5 Dominant	(notation) 1 Tonic, 4 Subdominant, 5 Dominant
A minor	(notation) 1 Tonic, 4 Subdominant, 5 Dominant	(notation) 1 Tonic, 4 Subdominant, 5 Dominant

DON'T FORGET

Tonic, subdominant and dominant notes can appear in different octaves.

IDENTIFYING CHORDS

For Higher Music, you will also need to be able to identify chords in major and minor keys. The table below shows the common chords in each of the four keys; C major, G major, F major and A minor. Examples of the chords are shown in both treble and bass clefs. In each case the chord name is printed above each chord (e.g. C, F, G and Am). It is common practice to use the lowercase letter **m** to indicate a minor chord. Therefore, Am would be the abbreviation for the chord of A minor. The chord number is also shown below each chord (e.g. I, IV, V and VI). It is

common practice to use Roman numerals to indicate the number of a chord. This refers to the degree (or note) of the scale on which the chord is based. For example; in the key of C major the chord of C is called chord I because it is based on the first note of the scale, the chord of F is called chord IV because it is based on the fourth note of the scale, the chord of G is called chord V because it is based on the fifth note of the scale, and the chord of Am (A minor) is called chord VI because it is based on the sixth note of the scale.

Key	Chord I, V, IV and VI in the treble clef	Chord I, V, IV and VI in the bass clef
C major	C(I) F(IV) G(V) Am(VI)	C(I) F(IV) G(V) Am(VI)
G major	G(I) C(IV) D(V) Em(VI)	G(I) C(IV) D(V) Em(VI)
F major	F(I) Bb(IV) C(V) Dm(VI)	F(I) Bb(IV) C(V) Dm(VI)
A minor	Am(I) Dm(IV) E(V) F(VI)	Am(I) Dm(IV) E(V) F(VI)

ONLINE

Find out more on identifying chords on the Digital Zone.

DON'T FORGET

It is common practice to use Roman numerals to indicate the number of a chord: I, IV, V and VI.

Remember that the notes of the chords may appear in different octaves and in different positions on the stave. For example, a chord containing the notes C, E and G will still be the chord of C even if the notes appear in a different order.

 THINGS TO DO AND THINK ABOUT

If you are asked to identify two or more chords, all the chords must be correct in order to gain the mark.

ONLINE TEST

Test yourself on Music Literacy at www.brightredbooks.net

59

RHYTHM AND TEMPO

GROUPINGS IN COMPOUND TIME

You should already be aware of note values such as the semibreve, minim, dotted minim, crotchet, dotted crotchet, quaver, dotted quaver and semiquaver. You should also be familiar with rhythmic groupings, including paired quavers and grouped semiquavers, in simple time.

For Higher Music, you will also need to be aware of note values and rhythmic groupings within three different time signatures in compound time: 6/8, 9/8 and 12/8. In these examples of compound time each beat is divided into three quavers as the beat is a dotted crotchet.

The table shows how these time signatures would appear at the beginning of a piece of music, along with a description of the time signature.

Time signature	Description
$\frac{6}{8}$	Two dotted crotchet beats in every bar
$\frac{9}{8}$	Three dotted crotchet beats in every bar
$\frac{12}{8}$	Four dotted crotchet beats in every bar

Here are examples of common rhythmic groupings for each of these three time signatures. Remember that in each case the beat is a dotted crotchet.

TRIPLETS

A **triplet** is a group of three notes performed in the time of two. For Higher Music, you will need to be able to identify two kinds of triplets: **triplet quavers** and **triplet crotchets**.

Triplet quavers occur when three quavers are performed in the time of two quavers.

 would be performed in the time of ♪♪

Triplet crotchets occur when three crotchets are performed in the time of two crotchets.

♩♩♩ would be performed in the time of ♩ ♩

The sign in music notation to indicate a triplet is the number 3 written either above or below the middle note. A square bracket, or sometimes a curved line (like a slur), may also be added to indicate the notes forming the triplet rhythm. The use of a square bracket is not strictly necessary if the notes are beamed together, as is usually the case with triplet quavers. However, a square bracket should always be used to indicate triplet crotchets.

Depending on the direction of the note stems, and the context of the music, the triplet sign can appear either above or below the notes. Here are other examples of how triplet quavers might look:

Here are other examples of how triplet crotchets might look:

Here is an example of triplet quavers at the start of the melody *Amazing Grace*.

Here is an example of triplet crotches near the start of the *Reverie* by Debussy.

When one part, or line, of music plays in groups of three, while at the same time another part plays in groups of two, this is known as **three against two** (3 against 2).

RESTS

Music consists of both sounds and silences. Just as music notation shows how long notes last, it also needs to show how long silences last. Silences in music are shown using signs called rests. Every note value in music (such as a quaver, crotchet, dotted crotchet, minim, dotted minim or semibreve) has a corresponding sign (called a rest) indicating the equivalent length of silence.

A silence lasting for the length of a crotchet, for example, is shown in music notation by a sign called a crotchet rest. The standard form a crotchet rest, used in printed music, looks like this:

However, an acceptable alternative, which is often easier to write in handwritten music, is:

A silence lasting for the length of a quaver is shown in music notation by a sign called a quaver rest:

Notice that the quaver rest looks like a mirror image of the alternative crotchet rest.

The signs for a minim rest and a semibreve rest look very similar as they are attached to one of the lines of the stave.

The minim rest sits on top of the third line:

The semibreve rest hangs below the fourth line:

Take care to note the difference between the minim rest and a semibreve rest.

Just as notes can be dotted in music notation (adding half the value to the original note), rests can also be dotted, adding half the value to the rest. Therefore, it is possible to have a dotted crotchet rest or a dotted minim rest.

It is important to note, however, that a whole bar rest in any time signature is indicated by a semibreve rest. Therefore, a whole bar rest in 2/4, 3/4, 4/4, 6/8, 9/8 or 12/8 time would always be shown as:

The table shows all the rests you will need to know, along with the corresponding notes, and the number of beats each note and rest lasts for.

Note	Name	Length	Rest
𝅝	Semibreve	4 beats	
𝅗𝅥.	Dotted minim	3 beats	
𝅗𝅥	Minim	2 beats	
𝅘𝅥.	Dotted crotchet	1 ½ beats	or
𝅘𝅥	Crotchet	1 beat	or
𝅘𝅥𝅮	Quaver	½ beat	

 THINGS TO DO AND THINK ABOUT

Look at any music that you are currently playing or singing. As well as any dynamic markings, look out for any other expression or articulation markings such as accents, slurs, staccato markings or phrase marks. Consider how taking account of such markings might help you interpret the music and contribute to the mood and character of the performance.

DON'T FORGET

Every note value has a corresponding rest.

DON'T FORGET

A whole bar rest in any time signature is indicated by a semibreve rest.

DON'T FORGET

Articulation markings such as accents, slurs, staccato marks or phrase marks can be written either above or below the notes.

 ONLINE TEST

Test yourself on Music Literacy at www.brightredbooks.net

COMPOSING

Details of how the composing assignment will be assessed can be found in the Course Assessment section on pages 82–83. The advice offered here is intended to provide some suggestions as to how to approach composing.

WHERE TO START?

You have the freedom to compose a piece of music in any style or genre. While it can be beneficial to experiment with different styles and genres, you may wish to work within a style or genre that particularly interests you, or that you are already familiar with. You should also consider, at an early stage, the instruments or voices you might use, and what other resources will be available to you.

You may, for example, decide to compose a piece of music for an instrument that you play, or a combination of instruments that you are already familiar with. This means that the music you compose is more likely to be appropriate to the instrument(s).

Here are some possible starting points for you to consider.

If you play an instrument such as the piano, keyboard or guitar, you might decide to compose:

- a solo piece for your chosen instrument
- a piece for your chosen instrument along with another instrument
- a piece for your chosen instrument within an ensemble.

If you play an orchestral instrument, you might decide to compose a piece of music for:

- your chosen instrument along with an accompanying instrument
- a suitable ensemble that includes your chosen instrument; such as a woodwind group, brass band, wind band, string quartet or string ensemble.

If you are a singer, or are interested in song writing, you might decide to compose:

- a song with instrumental accompaniment (e.g. piano or guitar)
- a song for a band or a group
- a piece for a vocal ensemble or choir.

If you are interested in technology, you might decide to compose music using:

- multi-track recording techniques
- computer programmes for recording music or creating scores
- apps that enable you to create your own backing tracks or manipulate sounds.

Whatever music you choose to compose, remember that your composition must include at least **four** elements from melody, harmony, rhythm, timbre and structure, one of which must be **harmony**.

MELODY

In creating a melody, you might start off with some simple ideas that you could develop using techniques such as repetition or sequences. However, to add some more sophistication to your melody you could experiment with:

- modes – creating a melody using a particular mode
- adding ornaments – such as an acciaccatura or a mordent
- different scales – such as harmonic minor, melodic minor or whole-tone
- modulation to different keys – such as the relative minor or relative major.

DON'T FORGET

Make sure that you are aware of the technical capabilities of the instrument you are composing for.

DON'T FORGET

Remember that some orchestral instruments need to have music transposed into different keys, or written in different clefs.

DON'T FORGET

Make sure that you know the range and combination of voices you have available.

DON'T FORGET

If you use pre-recorded loops or samples, this must be done within the context of a wider composition and clearly show your own creative input.

HARMONY

Remember that harmony is an element that you must use in your composition. As well as using major and minor chords, or features such as broken chords, vamp or drone, you could experiment with:

- different chords – such as the added 6th, dominant 7th, diminished and diminished 7th

- different cadences – such as a plagal cadence or interrupted cadence
- modulation to different keys – such as the relative minor or relative major
- other harmonic devices – such as Tierce de Picardie or cluster.

RHYTHM

As well as using time signatures in simple time or compound time, and features such syncopation, dotted rhythms or rubato, you could experiment with:

- irregular time signatures – such as 5/4 or 7/4

- time changes – alternating between different time signatures
- different rhythmic groupings – such as triplets, 3 against 2, or cross rhythms
- other rhythmic devices – such as augmentation or diminution.

TIMBRE

Your exploration of timbre will depend on which combination of instruments or voices you are composing for, or which sounds you are using. If you are composing for a string instrument, you might use playing techniques such as arco, pizzicato or con sordino. A composition involving electric guitars may include effects such as reverb or distortion. Any composition could be

enhanced by using varied dynamics, or even a contrast between legato and staccato. However, you could also experiment with:

- playing techniques – such as tremolando or harmonics
- expression markings – such as accents, slurs or staccato
- electronic effects – such as distortion, reverb, pre-recorded loops, samples or Musique concrète techniques.

STRUCTURE

In experimenting with different structures, there are a wide range of forms and textures that you might wish to explore. These include:

- instrumental forms – such as binary (AB), ternary (ABA), rondo (ABACA) or theme and variations

- vocal forms– such as verse and chorus, strophic or through-composed
- more advanced forms – such as ritornello, passacaglia or sonata form
- different textures – such as contrapuntal/polyphonic or homophonic
- other structural features – such as Alberti bass, walking bass, ostinato/riff, imitation or coda.

IDEAS

As well as considering which concepts and musical features to include in your composition, you might also consider other factors that could influence your composition. For example, you may draw on ideas outwith music as a source of inspiration. Or, you might have a particular context in mind for composing music.

Drawing on possible sources of inspiration outwith music might include composing:

- music to convey a story or a poem
- a song, using the words of a poem for the lyrics
- music based on a painting or a series of pictures
- music inspired by a particular event
- a piece of music, or a song, to express particular feelings or emotions.

You could also consider particular contexts that require music to be composed, and set yourself the task of composing one of the following:

- background music for a film
- theme music for a television programme
- music for a video game
- incidental music for a play
- music for a special occasion, such as a concert or a religious service.

Whatever you choose as the inspiration or context for your composition, try to make your composition interesting and imaginative. Take care to structure your musical ideas in an organised way, so that your composition is coherent and musically convincing.

 THINGS TO DO AND THINK ABOUT

Compose for an instrument (or voice) that you are familiar with.

COURSE ASSESSMENT

THE QUESTION PAPER AND QUESTION STYLES

ASSESSMENT

The Higher Music course consists of four components, all of which are externally assessed.

This section will provide you with more detailed information about the components, along with advice on how to prepare for each of them.

The following table provides a summary of the four components, showing how each one will be assessed, the total number of marks available for each component, and the scaled mark:

Assessment

Component	How it will be assessed	Marks available	Scaled mark
Question Paper	Written examination based on listening to excerpts of music	40	35%
Composing Assignment	Submission of a completed composition (20 marks) and a composing review (10 marks)	30	15%
Performance Instrument 1	Live performance marked by a visiting assessor	30	25%
Performance Instrument 2	Live performance marked by a visiting assessor	30	25%

The course assessment will provide the basis for the final grade awarded (for example, A, B, C or D). Your grade will be based on the total percentage for all four course assessment components added together (i.e. the scaled marks for Question Paper, the Composing Assignment and Performance on both instruments, or one instrument and voice).

This Higher Music Study Guide provides you with a range of practical activities to help develop your kills in Listening, Composing and Performing, and practical advice about preparing for the Question Paper, the Composing Assignment and the Performance Exam.

OVERVIEW OF THE QUESTION PAPER

You will have a final written exam in the form of a question paper. The question paper, which will last approximately one hour, is based on listening to excerpts of music and answering questions on what you hear. The question paper is marked out of 40, and will then be scaled to a mark out of 35, meaning that it will be worth 35% of your course award.

The purpose of the question paper is to test your knowledge and understanding of music concepts and music literacy. You will demonstrate your knowledge and understanding of music concepts by answering questions based on a variety of excerpts from different styles of music. A range of question types will be used in the question paper, covering a variety of music concepts including music literacy. All the questions in the question paper are compulsory.

This section will provide you with advice on how to revise for the question paper. It will also you show examples of the types of questions you will come across in the question paper, along with some tips on how to go about answering the questions.

TOPICS TO REVISE

The questions in the exam will test your knowledge and understanding of music concepts from styles that you have covered throughout your course, such as:

- Baroque music (Basso continuo, Concerto grosso, Ritornello, Passacaglia, Ripieno and Concertino)
- Classical and Romantic music (Sonata, Chamber music, String quartet, Sonata form, Exposition and Subject)
- Twentieth-century music (Impressionist and Musique concrète)
- Vocal music (Recitative, Lied, Da capo aria, Coloratura and Through-composed)
- Sacred music (Plainchant, Mass and Oratorio)
- Instrumental music and playing techniques (Tremolando and Harmonics)
- Popular music styles (Jazz funk and Soul).

Questions in the Higher Music question paper may also draw on topics that would have been covered at National 3, National 4 and National 5, such as:

- Scottish Music
- World Music.

Some of the questions in the exam will also test your knowledge and understanding of other aspects of music, including:

- identifying specific musical instruments or instrumental groups
- playing techniques used by different instruments
- Italian terms (for tempo, dynamics and playing techniques)
- music literacy.

DON'T FORGET

The Higher Music question paper may also test your knowledge and understanding of music concepts from N3, N4 and N5 levels.

QUESTION STYLES

The questions in the exam will be in a wide variety of formats, including:

- multiple choice questions, choosing concepts from a range of options
- writing short answers (single words or short phrases)
- following a music guide and inserting appropriate concepts
- music literacy (involving music notation and identifying chord changes)
- identifying prominent concepts in a piece of music under given headings
- comparing two excerpts of music and identifying concepts common to both
- identifying concepts in a vocal piece at the appropriated places in the text.

The number of marks available for each question will be indicated at the right-hand side of the page of the question paper.

In this section you will see examples of how these questions will look, along with advice on how to answer them.

ONLINE

Head to the BrightRED Digital Zone for a link to the SQA Past Papers.

THINGS TO DO AND THINK ABOUT

You can access Higher Music past papers and marking instructions from the Music subject page of the SQA website.

This will enable you to see exactly what questions have been asked in the Higher Music question paper over the last few years, and will help you become more familiar with the layout of the question paper.

MULTIPLE CHOICE QUESTIONS

MULTIPLE CHOICE QUESTIONS

Multiple choice questions simply ask you to identify concepts that you hear in the music, chosen from a given list.

There will be a variety of multiple choice questions, asking you to:

- select **one** correct answer from **four** options
- select **three** correct answer from **nine** options
- select **four** correct answer from **ten** options.

In most multiple choice questions, you will be expected to write your answers on the lines below the list of concepts.

Select *one* correct answer from *four* options

Listen to this excerpt and tick (✓) **one** box to describe the chord outlined.

The music will be played **twice**.

☐ Dominant 7th   ☐ Added 6th

☐ Diminished 7th   ☐ Minor

Here is the music for the first time.

Here is the music for the second time.

DON'T FORGET

Remember to tick only **one box** for this question.

In this question you are simply required to tick one box to identify the appropriate concept. Remember to only tick **one box**. Here are some tips to help you answer this type of question.

- Read over the concepts, trying to anticipate what each might sound like.
- Take note of how many times you are going to hear the music.
- If you are not sure of the correct answer, try to eliminate the concepts that are definitely not present. This will help you to narrow your options.
- If you tick an incorrect concept by mistake, simply cross out the incorrect answer and tick the correct one. Just make it clear which concept you are choosing.

Select *three* correct answer from *nine* options

DON'T FORGET

Check how many concepts you have been asked to identify, and listen out for concepts that might be related. There is one mark available for each correct answer.

This question features vocal music.

Listen to this excerpt and identify **three** concepts in the music from those listed below.

Read through the concepts before hearing the music.

Da capo aria	Pizzicato	Plagal cadence
Recitative	Obligato	Alberti bass
Oratorio	Tierce de Picardie	Soprano

The music will be played **twice** with a pause of 10 seconds between playings, and a pause of 40 seconds before the next question starts.

contd

Give your **three** answers on the lines below.

_____

_____

_____

Here is the music for the first time.

Here is the music for the second time.

Select *four* correct answer from *ten* options.

This question features instrumental music.

Listen to this excerpt and identify **four** concepts in the music from those listed below.

Read through the concepts before hearing the music.

Symphony	Concerto grosso
String quartet	Ritornello
Passacaglia	Coloratura
Ripieno	Time changes
Con sordino	Triplets

The music will be played **twice** with a pause of 10 seconds between playings, and a pause of 40 seconds before the next question starts.

Give your **four** answers on the lines below.

_____

_____

_____

_____

Here is the music for the first time.

Here is the music for the second time.

Here is the music for the third time.

In these questions you are required to identify a specified number of concepts from a given list. You should then write the correct concepts on the lines below the list. Here are some tips to help you answer this type of question.

- Read the question carefully to make sure you know how many concepts you are required to identify. It will either be three or four.

- Take note of how many times you are going to hear the music. When identifying three concepts you will hear the music twice. When identifying four concepts you will hear the music three times.

- When asked to identify **three** or **four** concepts, it can be helpful to consider which concepts might be related (i.e. which combination of concepts are likely to be found in the same piece or style of music). It might also be helpful to consider which concepts are not related (i.e. a combination of concepts that would be unlikely to be found in the same piece or style of music). This would help to avoid choosing inappropriate combinations of concepts that are clearly unrelated.

- If you are not sure of the correct answers, try to eliminate any concepts that are definitely not present. This will help you to narrow your options.

- You might find it helpful to tick or underline correct concepts as you hear them, or cross out concepts that you know are not present.

- You must remember to write your answers on the lines below the list of concepts.

- If you write an incorrect concept by mistake, simply cross out the incorrect answer and write the correct one. Just make it clear which concepts you are identifying.

 THINGS TO DO AND THINK ABOUT

When answering multiple choice questions, think about which concepts might be related and are likely to be found in the same piece or style of music.

 ONLINE

Head to www.brightredbooks.net for a link to the SQA past papers and marking instructions.

MUSIC GUIDE AND WRITING SHORT ANSWERS

MUSIC GUIDE

In this question, you will be asked to identify features of a piece of music in the order

they occur in the music. A guide to the music will laid out for you to follow. You will see that further information is required and you should insert this in each of the areas that have been left blank.

There will be a pause of 30 seconds to allow you to read through the question. The music will then be played three times, with a pause of 20 seconds between playings.

In the first two playings, a voice will help guide you through the music (saying; "1 – 2 – 3 – 4 – 5" at the appropriate points in the music). There is no voice in the third playing.

In this question you will hear instrumental music.

A guide to the music is shown below. You are required to complete this guide by inserting music concepts.

There will now be a pause of 30 seconds to allow you to read through the question.

The music will be played **three** times, with a pause of 20 seconds between playings. You will then have a further 30 seconds to complete your answer.

In the first two playings, a voice will help guide you through the music.

There is no voice in the third playing.

Here is the music for the first time.

Here is the music for the second time.

Here is the music for the third time.

1. The instrument playing the melody is a/an
   _____

2. The ornament featured is a/an
   _____

3. The playing technique used by the accompanying instrument is
   _____ (Italian term)

4. The melody features a descending
   _____ scale.

5. The cadence is
   _____

DON'T FORGET

Each answer must be a music concept, from any level: National 3, National 4, National 5 or Higher. There is one mark available for each correct answer.

contd

Here are some tips to help you answer this type of question.

- Read the statements in the guide carefully. The wording will help you focus on possible answers before even hearing the music.

- Follow the guide carefully while the music is playing.

- Pay particular attention to where the numbers are read out by the voice during the first and second playings of the music.

- Each answer you write must be a music concept.

- Sometimes the correct answer will be an Italian term.

- There may be more than one possible answer.

- In this question, the correct answers could be concepts from National 3, National 4, National 5 or Higher.

WRITING SHORT ANSWERS (SINGLE WORDS OR SHORT PHRASES)

Some questions will require you to write one or two words or a short phrase.

In these types of questions, you will not be given a list of concepts to choose from. Instead, you will need to identify the concept yourself by listening to the music.

It is important to note that in this type of question the answer **must** be a concept introduced at **Higher** level. For example; if you are asked to identify an ornament in the music, the answer would have to be either **acciaccatura** or **mordent** as these are both **Higher** concepts. Neither **grace note** nor **trill** would be acceptable answers because they are both National 5 concepts.

(a) Listen to the following excerpt and identify the playing technique used by the solo instrument.

_____

(b) Listen to a continuation of the previous excerpt and identify the ornament.

_____

(c) Listen to another excerpt and identify the style of the music.

_____

(d) Listen to a new excerpt. Identify the cadence at the end.

_____

DON'T FORGET

In questions that require you to write one or two words or a short phrase, the answer must be a Higher level concept.

THINGS TO DO AND THINK ABOUT

When completing the Music Guide, remember that your answers can be music concepts from any level: National 3, National 4, National 5 or Higher.

When answering questions that require you to write one or two words, or a short phrase, the answer must be a Higher concept.

MUSIC LITERACY

QUESTION FORMAT

In music literacy questions, you will be asked to answer questions relating to printed music. You will hear the music four times. On the first hearing you should listen carefully to the excerpt while you follow the music. Do not attempt to write anything during the first playing. Just familiarise yourself with the music – both how it sounds and what it looks like on the printed page.

Remember that some of the notes, rhythms, bar lines, rests, time signature or key signature might be missing.

You will then have two minutes to read over the question and see exactly what you are going to be asked to do. There will be approximately six parts to this question; (a), (b), (c), (d), (e) and (f); each of which carries one mark.

The music will then be played three more times with a pause of 30 seconds between playings. After the final playing, you will have two minutes before the next question starts, during which time you should make sure that you have completed all parts of the question.

There are a number of different things you could be asked to do in this question, many of which require a knowledge and understanding of music notation, such as:

- name the key of the music

- insert the key signature at the correct place

- insert the time signature at the correct place

- describe an interval formed between two notes

- write an interval above a given note in the treble clef

- complete missing notes – the rhythm would be printed above the stave

- insert a missing accidental in front of a particular note

- insert a missing rest from a particular bar

- correct the rhythm in a particular group of notes

- identify the total value of a note, which may include a tied note

- insert missing bar lines

- identify chords, using either letter names or numbers

- identify tonic, subdominant and dominant notes

- transpose notes from treble clef down **one octave** into the bass clef, using the given blank stave

- add particular signs, symbols or performance directions to the printed music

- identify where a particular feature occurs in the music.

SOME HELPFUL TIPS

Here are some tips to help you answer different types of music literacy questions:

- When naming the key of the music you will only be expected to identify the keys of C major, G major, F major and A minor. Make sure you know the key signatures for these keys.

- The key signature should appear that the start of every stave.

- The time signature should appear only at the beginning of the music, immediately after the key signature. The time signature consists of two numbers, one above the other, and should not be written as a fraction. Make sure that you know the difference between time signatures in simple time and compound time.

- In describing an interval formed between two notes always count from the lower note to the higher note. The only intervals you will be required to identify will be a 2nd, 3rd, 4th, 5th, 6th, 7th or octave.

- When writing an interval above a given note in the treble clef, always count from the lower note to the higher note. The only intervals you will be required to write will be a 2nd, 3rd, 4th, 5th, 6th, 7th or octave.

- When completing missing notes, care should be taken to ensure that any music notation is clear and unambiguous. Make sure that note heads are written clearly on the appropriate lines or in the appropriate spaces.

- When inserting a missing accidental, take care to use the correct sign: flat, sharp or natural. Also, remember that the accidental comes before the note head and should be written clearly on the appropriate line or in the appropriate space.

- When inserting a missing rest from a particular bar, make sure that the bar adds up to the appropriate number of beats. Also, make sure that you know how to group notes and rests in both simple time and compound time.

contd

- When correcting the rhythm of a particular group of notes, be aware that rhythmic groupings may include dotted rhythms or triplets, as well as groupings in either simple time or compound time.

- When identifying the total value of a note, this may include dotted notes or tied notes.

- When inserting missing bar lines take care to note if the music is in simple time or compound time. Also, remember that some notes may be tied across bars.

- When identifying chords, you can use either chord letter names or numbers. Chord letter names would be in the form of guitar chord names printed above the stave, e.g. in the key of G major that would be G, C, D and Em (E minor). When using chord numbers, the convention is to use Roman Numerals: I, IV, V and VI. Listen carefully to the bass notes (i.e. the lowest notes) as the bass note is often the root note of the chord. Looking carefully at the notes of the melody may also give you a clue as to which chords are used, as melody notes are often contained within the chords. If you are asked to identify two or more chords, all the chords must be correct in order to gain the mark.

- When identifying tonic, subdominant and dominant notes, this would be restricted to the keys of C major, G major, F major and A minor. Make sure that you are able to identify tonic, subdominant and dominant notes in theses keys.

- When transposing notes from the treble clef down **one octave** into the bass clef, write the notes on the given blank stave. In order to gain the mark both the pitch and rhythm of each note must be correct. Each note must have the majority of note head in the correct place (i.e. on the correct line or in the correct space) and note heads must be appropriately filled in. Any accidentals must also be correctly placed before the appropriate note.

- Adding signs, symbols or performance directions to the printed music might involve inserting repeat signs, 1st and 2nd time endings, phrase marks, slurs, accents, staccato or dynamic markings.

- When identifying where a particular feature occurs in the music, you may be required to annotate the printed music in some way to indicate where you hear a feature. Examples of this might include:

  Write the letter 'T' above the bar where you hear a timpani roll.

  Write the letter 'C' above the stave where the countermelody on the oboe begins.

  Write 'X' above the note where you hear a mordent.

  Write 'P' above the stave where you hear a plagal cadence.

It will be possible to answer some parts of this question without actually hearing the music, e.g. naming the key of music, inserting the key signature, describing an interval, inserting a missing rest or inserting missing bar lines, identifying the value of a note, or transposing notes down **one octave** from the treble clef into the bass clef.

However, for some of the questions you will need to follow the music very carefully, e.g. inserting missing notes, rhythms or accidentals, identifying chords, or identifying where a particular feature occurs in the music.

During the one minute that you have to read over the question, you might find it helpful to decide which parts of the question you will be able to answer without hearing the music, and which parts can only be answered by following the music. This will help focus your listening on those particular parts of the question that need you to follow the music during the three further playings. The parts of the question that don't require you to hear the music can then be completed during the two minutes that you have at the end.

 THINGS TO DO AND THINK ABOUT

When answering questions involving music literacy, think about which parts of the question you might be able to answer without hearing the music and which parts can only be answered by hearing the music. This will help you focus on what you actually need to listen for.

 DON'T FORGET

Decide which parts of the question you will be able to answer without hearing the music and which parts can only be answered by following the music.

IDENTIFYING PROMINENT CONCEPTS

INTRODUCTION

In this question you will be asked to identify prominent concepts in the music.

You should identify at least **two** concepts from each of **three** given headings. The headings are taken from the concepts lists and could include any combination of the following:

- style
- melody
- harmony
- rhythm
- tempo

- texture
- structure
- form
- timbre
- dynamics (including Italian terms).

You will hear the music three times.

You may use the table for rough working, but your **final answer must be written on the appropriate page**.

The music will be played three times.

This question is based on instrumental music.

In this question you should identify the most prominent concepts which are present in the music.

As you listen, identify at least **two** concepts from each of the following headings.

Melody/Harmony   Rhythm   Timbre

You will hear the music **three times** and you should make notes as you listen.

Rough work will not be marked.

Marks will only be awarded for the final answer.

After the third playing you will have three minutes to write your final answer in the space provided.

Here is the music for the first time.

Here is the music for the second time.

Here is the music for the third time.

Melody/harmony	
Rhythm	
Timbre	

Your final answer must be written on the appropriate page. An example of this is on the next page.

contd

Final answer

_____

_____

_____

_____

_____

_____

_____

_____

_____

_____

_____

Here are some tips to help you answer this question.

- Make brief notes as you listen in the *Rough work* section.

- Listen out for the most **prominent concepts** and don't try to write down everything that you hear.

- Try to identify at least **two prominent concepts** under each of the **three** headings.

- Be aware that the headings provided may change from year to year, and that the headings used could be any combination of headings from the tables of music concepts.

- Remember to write your final answer on the page that says *Final answer*.

When writing your final answer you may choose any of the following approaches.

- Writing your answer in sentences.

- Writing concepts as a list, or bullet points.

- Listing concepts under the headings provided.

If writing lists of concepts, remember that the question is asking you to identify the most **prominent** concepts in the music. It is important, therefore, not to write long lists of concepts unrelated to the music, or extensive lists of contradictory concepts. This approach would not answer the question correctly and may result in you incurring a penalty.

If you choose to copy the headings and then write the concepts under the headings, there will be no penalty if you mistakenly write correct concepts under the incorrect headings. The important thing is to identify the correct **prominent** concepts. There is no penalty for writing incorrect concepts, as long as you don't write an extensive lists of contradictory concepts. Remember that your *rough work* will not be marked. Marks will only be awarded for your final answer.

 **DON'T FORGET**

Try to identify at least **two prominent concepts** under each of the **three** given headings. Avoid writing long lists of contradictory or unrelated concepts.

 THINGS TO DO AND THINK ABOUT

You can access Higher Music past papers and marking instructions from the Music subject page of the SQA website.

This will enable you to see exactly what questions have been asked in the Higher Music question paper over the last few years, and will help you become more familiar with the layout of the question paper.

COMPARISON

COMPARING TWO EXCERPTS OF MUSIC

This question involves listening to two excerpts of music and identifying concepts common to both.

In this question you compare two excerpts of music.

You must first identify concepts present in each excerpt and then decide which **five** concepts are common to both excerpts. Both excerpts will be played **three** times, with a pause of 10 seconds between playings.

As you listen, tick (✓) boxes in **Column A** and **Column B** to identify what you hear in Excerpt 1 and Excerpt 2. **These columns are for rough work only and will not be marked**.

After the music has been played **three** times you will be given two minutes to decide which concepts are common to both excerpts and to tick **five** boxes in **Column C**.

You will have one minute to read through the question.

Here is Excerpt 1 for the first time. **Remember to tick (✓) concepts in Column A.**

Here is Excerpt 2 for the first time. **Remember to tick (✓) concepts in Column B.**

Here is Excerpt 1 for the second time.

Here is Excerpt 2 for the second time.

Here is Excerpt 1 for the third time.

Here is Excerpt 2 for the third time.

You now have two minutes to identify the **five** concepts common to both excerpts.

Remember to tick (✓) five boxes only in Column C.

	Concepts	Column A Excerpt 1	Column B Excerpt 2	Column C 5 concepts common to
Style	Baroque			
	Classical			
	Romantic			
	Impressionist			
Melody/ Harmony	Perfect cadence			
	Acciaccatura			
	Modulation to the relative major			
	Chromatic scale			
Rhythm	Rubato			
	Triplets			
	Time changes			
	Compound time			
Timbre / Dynamics	Tremolando			
	Harmonics			
	Con sordino			
	Pizzicato			
				5 marks

contd

Here are some tips to help you answer this question.

- Read through the concepts carefully before hearing the music.

- Try to anticipate how you would recognise the concepts.

- During Excerpt 1, remember to tick concepts in Column A.

- During Excerpt 2, remember to tick concepts in Column B.

- If you are not sure of the correct concepts, try to eliminate the concepts that are definitely not present.

- You might find it helpful to place crosses in Column A and Column B against the concepts which are not present in each of the excerpts.

- Finally, remember to tick five concepts only in Column C to indicate the five concepts common to both excerpts.

- If you tick an incorrect concept by mistake, simply cross out the incorrect tick and tick the correct concept. Just make it clear which concepts you are identifying.

 DON'T FORGET

Remember to tick (✓) five boxes only in Column C to identify the five concepts common to both excerpts.

LYRICS/TEXT QUESTION

In this question you will listen to part of a song or a choral piece, while following the words.

You will also be given a list of features which occur in the music.

The lyrics of the song, or the words of a choral piece, will be printed in the left-hand column in a table on the opposite page. You will be required to insert each feature once in the column on the right at the point where it occurs.

An example of how this question looks can be found on the Digital Zone.

Here are some tips to help you answer this question.

- Read through the list of features carefully before hearing the music.

- Notice that some of the feature may combine two concepts.

- You only need to write the word that is underlined.

- You should only insert each feature once.

- Some feature may occur more than one. So, take note if you are being asked to identify the first example of a particular feature.

- More than one feature could occur in the same place in the music. In this situation, you would insert more than one concept on the same line.

- If you write a feature in the wrong place by mistake, simply cross it out and write the feature in the correct place. Just make it clear which feature you are identifying in which place.

ONLINE

See an example of how this question looks on the Digital Zone.

DON'T FORGET

Remember to insert each feature once only.

 THINGS TO DO AND THINK ABOUT

When comparing two excerpts of music, try to eliminate concepts that are definitely not present in either excerpt. This will help to narrow your options for the concepts that are common to both excerpts.

When answering the question with lyrics or text, you might find it helpful to cross out each feature as you identify it. This will allow you to see exactly which features are left.

COMPOSING ASSIGNMENT 1

OVERVIEW

The purpose of the composing assignment is to provide you with opportunities to explore and develop musical ideas to create music. The assignment has two parts:

- composing one piece of music
- reviewing the composing process.

Your composition may be in any style or genre and must last a minimum of 1 minute and a maximum of 3½ minutes.

The submission of your composing assignment must include all of the following:

- an audio recording of your composition
- a score or performance plan of your composition
- a composing review.

Your composing assignment should demonstrate the following skills, knowledge and understanding:

- planning and reviewing your own music
- exploring and developing musical ideas
- creating music which is original to you.

In preparing your composing assignment it is important to note the following.

- An arrangement of your own or someone else's music is not acceptable.
- Your composition may contain sections of improvisation, but this must be in the context of a wider composition which demonstrates composing skills. A piece of music which is solely an improvisation is not acceptable.
- If you choose to work with pre-recorded loops this must also be done within the context of a wider composition and show the compositional process. Your own creative input must be clearly identifiable.

COMPOSING ASSIGNMENT TASK

For the composing assignment, you are required to:

- plan the assignment

- explore and develop musical ideas using at least **four** elements from melody, harmony, rhythm, timbre and structure, one of which must be **harmony**
- create one complete piece of music.

PLAN, EXPLORE, DEVELOP AND CREATE

During the process of working on your composition you are encouraged to plan, explore, develop and create. This will help you to focus on the process of composing music and prepare your composing review.

Plan

In planning your composition you should consider the following questions.

- What kind of music you would like to create?
- Do you want to compose within a particular style or genre that interests you, or do you want to experiment with composing music in different styles or genres?
- Which instruments, voices or sounds would you like to use?
- Will you use a particular structure such as ABA, rondo, verse and chorus, or theme and variations?

- How will you keep a record of the decisions that you make?

Explore

In exploring ideas for your composition you should:

- start with simple ideas – you can develop or add to them later
- experiment with musical ideas using at least four of the following elements: melody, harmony, rhythm, timbre or structure, one of which must be **harmony**
- experiment with different chords or chord progressions
- reflect on your composing, considering which of your musical ideas are most effective
- keep a record of how you have explored and experimented with musical ideas.

contd

Develop

In developing ideas for your composition you might:

- change some of the musical ideas you have been exploring and experimenting with
- discard some ideas that you don't think are working so well
- extend some of your musical ideas to make your composition more imaginative
- add more concepts or musical features to make your composition more interesting
- keep a record of the ways in which you have explored and developed your musical ideas.

COMPOSING REVIEW

As well as composing music, you will also need to submit a composing review. The composing review will provide a clear account of your composing process, showing that you have:

- planned your composition
- explored and developed musical ideas using at least **four** elements from melody, harmony, rhythm, timbre and structure, one of which must be **harmony**

Create

In creating for your final composition you should:

- decide which of your musical ideas work best
- use your best musical ideas to create your composition
- remember that your composition must include harmony or chords
- create a score or a performance plan for your composition
- make an audio recording of your composition
- identify the strengths of your composition and consider any areas which night be improved.

- created one complete piece of music.

Your composing review must include a detailed account of:

- the main decisions you have made
- how you have explored and developed your musical ideas
- the main strengths of your composition and/or anything that could be improved.

THINGS TO DO AND THINK ABOUT

- Compose for an instrument (or voice) that you are familiar with.
- Keep a record of how you explore and experiment with your musical ideas.
- Reflect on your composing, considering which of your musical ideas are most effective.
- Consider how you will create a score or a performance plan for your composition.
- Consider how you will make an audio recording of your composition.

DON'T FORGET

Keep a record of the main decisions that you make so that you can come back to that for your composing review.

DON'T FORGET

You must use the SQA composing review template which is available from the SQA Higher Music subject page.

ONLINE

You can also find a composing review template, with guidance notes, available at www.brightredbooks.net/HigherMusic.

77

COMPOSING ASSIGNMENT 2

SCORE OR PERFORMANCE PLAN

One of the requirements of your composing assignment is that you create either a score or a performance plan for your composition. A score would involve using your knowledge of music literacy to notate the appropriate notes and rhythms for your composition. This could be either handwritten, or printed using any music notation software.

Your score should also include all the information required for someone else to be able perform or follow your composition. This would include:

- identifying any instrument(s) or voice(s) used
- notes written on the stave or staves
- accurate indication of note values, rhythms and rhythmic groupings
- key signature(s) as appropriate
- time signature(s) as appropriate
- bars and bar lines
- tempo indications
- dynamic markings as appropriate
- appropriate signs and symbols such as repeat signs or first and second time endings
- performance directions relevant to the instrument(s) or voice(s) used, such as arco, pizzicato, con sordino, a cappella or phrase marks
- any other appropriate performance directions, such as slurs, accents or staccato markings.

In some styles or genres of music, it may not be appropriate to produce a conventional score that uses standard music notation. This might be the case if your composition uses elements of improvisation, is computer based, or uses element of electronic music or Musique concrète. In such cases you may decide to create a performance plan instead. A performance plan is a visual representation of your composition that would clearly indicate what is happening in the music. Although a performance plan may not include any conventional music notation, it still needs to act a guide to the music. This means that the performance plan would need to clearly identify:

- the overall structure of the music
- any instrument(s) or voice(s) used
- playing or performing techniques used by any instrument(s) or voice(s)
- music concepts or other techniques used in the composition
- how the concepts are used or combined
- any effects used, including electronic or digital effects
- any other features relevant to the music.

In identifying the overall structure of the music, you may refer to particular sections of your composition using heading such as:

- Introduction
- Verse 1/Section A
- Chorus/Section B

DON'T FORGET

Create a score or performance plan for your composition, as well as an audio recording.

DON'T FORGET

The score for your composing assignment needs to contain all the information required for someone else to perform or interpret your music.

ONLINE

You can also find music manuscript paper, with various templates, at www.brightredbooks.net/HigherMusic

contd

- Middle 8/Section C

- Verse 2

- Chorus

- Coda.

If your composition has been created using a music application, rather than conventional instruments or voices, you may wish to include some screenshots in your performance plan. If you do include screenshots you must take care to explain what the screenshots represent in the music.

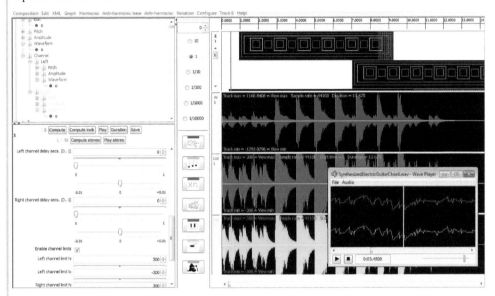

AUDIO RECORDING

No matter what style or genre you have chosen for your composition, you are required to submit an audio recording so that whoever is assessing your composition can listen to it.

You may use any recording equipment available to you. However, in creating an audio recording of your composition, you must make sure that you choose an appropriate audio format for your final recording. You will need to be confident that anyone will be able to listen to your audio recording, irrespective of the device they are using to play it.

If you have used a specific music application to create your composition, you may need to export your work to a universal file type, such as MP3, so that anyone will be able to listen to it.

 THINGS TO DO AND THINK ABOUT

Once you have created your final audio recording, try playing it on more than one device to make sure that it works properly.

COMPOSING ASSIGNMENT 3

ASSESSMENT OF THE COMPOSING ASSIGNMENT

Your composition must use at least **four** of the following musical elements, of which one must be harmony:

- melody
- structure
- harmony
- timbre.
- rhythm

The following table provides some examples of what a good Higher composition might include, within each of these elements, as well as some common faults that you should be trying to avoid.

Composing music	What a good composition might include:	Some common faults to be avoided:
Melody	An interesting melodic shape, with a variety of steps and leaps.	A repetitive or disjointed melody.
	Use of ornaments as appropriate to enhance and develop the melody.	No melodic decoration or development.
	Shows an understanding of scales or scale patterns or modes (e.g. major, harmonic minor, melodic minor whole-tone, chromatic, pentatonic or modal).	Shows little understanding of scales, scale patterns or modes.
	Addition of a countermelody, descant or obbligato to add interest.	Little evidence of melodic devices such as a countermelody, descant or obligato.
	Using a variety melodic devices such as question and answer, sequence, drone, pedal, inverted pedal or glissando.	A limited range of melodic devices, or over-using a particular melodic device.
Harmony	Using a variety of chords, possibly including the dominant 7th, diminished 7th or added 6th.	Using a limited range of chords
	A chord progression that is interesting and convincing.	Inappropriate combination of chords.
	Using broken chord or arpeggio patterns to add interest.	Only using block chords.
	Use of modulation, from a major key to the relative minor or from a minor key to the relative major.	Little variety of keys or little understanding of modulation.
	Using cadences in an appropriate and musically convincing way.	Showing little understanding of cadences.
Rhythm	Using a variety of rhythms and rhythmic grouping, including triplets or 3 against 2.	Limited use of rhythms and little rhythmic variety.
	Using irregular time signatures, time signatures in compound time, or time changes.	Keeping to the same time signature with little rhythmic interest or variety.
	Using a variety of rhythmic devices such as augmentation, or diminution in appropriate and musically convincing ways.	A limited range of rhythmic devices, or over-using a particular rhythmic device.
Timbre	Using a variety of instruments or combining instrumental sounds in imaginative ways.	Using one instrument only, with little variety in tone or dynamics.
	Using a variety of playing techniques as appropriate to different instruments, e.g. arco and pizzicato strings, finger-picking and strumming the guitar, or using effects such as reverb or distortion.	Using a limited range of playing techniques, or not exploring the playing techniques possible on a particular instrument.
	Using slurs, accents or staccato marks to add interest to articulation in the music.	Little or no variety in articulation.
Structure	Organising your ideas in a systematic and musically convincing way.	Having musical ideas in a disjointed way with little sense of organisation.
	Using a clear structure such as ternary form, rondo form, verse and chorus, theme and variations or sonata form.	Having little sense of a thought-out structure.
	Using a range of structural devices appropriate to the style such as passacaglia, walking bass, Alberti bass, strophic or through-composed.	Using a limited range of structural devices or not using them in an appropriate or musically convincing way.
	Including structural features such as exposition, subject or coda.	A limited range of structural features, displaying little contrast.
	Developing the music by using contrasting homophonic, polyphonic or contrapuntal textures.	Little contrast and limited use of different textures.
	Using phrase marks to indicate an understanding of structure.	No indication, or understanding, of phrases.

contd

For the composing review, you are also required to:

- provide a detailed account of the main decisions you made when exploring and developing your musical ideas

- identify strengths and/or areas which may be improved.

The following table shows the different areas that will be used in assessing your composing review. It also provides a summary of what would be good to include in your composing review, as well as some common faults that you should be trying to avoid.

Composing review	What a good composing review might include:	Some common faults to be avoided:
Main decisions made	A detailed account of the main decisions made. A clear explanation of how you planned your composition.	A limited account of the main decisions made. Little evidence of planning.
Exploration and development of musical ideas	A detailed account of the exploration and development of musical ideas. Identifying the concepts you have used in an organised way. Indicating how you have experimented with compositional methods and developed your musical ideas. Showing that you have considered different possibilities.	A limited explanation of the exploration and development of musical ideas. Simply listing concepts with little sense of organisation. Little explanation as to how you have experimented with compositional methods or developed your musical ideas. Little consideration given to different possibilities.
Strengths and/or areas for improvement	Clear identification of strengths and/or areas for improvement. Identifying clearly what works well in your composition, with particular reference to musical ideas and compositional methods. Identifying clearly that you could do to improve your composition, with reference to musical ideas and compositional methods.	Limited identification of strengths and/or areas for improvement. Showing little understanding of what works well in your composition, or limited reference to musical ideas or compositional methods. Showing little awareness of what you could do to improve your composition, or limited reference to musical ideas and compositional methods.

 THINGS TO DO AND THINK ABOUT

Maintain a record of the different stages in the process of your composition, making sure that you keep a detailed account of:

- the main decisions you have made in planning your composition

- the composing process, showing clearly how you have explored and developed musical ideas and used different compositional methods

- reflecting on your work, identifying what you consider to be the main strengths of your composition, or areas that would improve your composition.

 DON'T FORGET

You must include at least two points about either strengths or areas for improvement in the composing review.

COMPOSING ASSIGNMENT 4

MARKS

The composing assignment has a total of 30 marks (scaled to 15% of the overall course award).

Separate marks are awarded for each part of the composing assignment.

Marks are awarded as follows:

- composing music (20 marks)
- composing review (10 marks).

The following table shows a breakdown of the mark range from 0–20, along with the related composing music summary statements, that will be used to assess your composition:

Mark range	Composing music summary statements
18–20	An excellent composition demonstrating a range of musical ideas which have been developed imaginatively and convincingly – appropriate to your chosen style. The selection and use of elements is highly creative and effective.
15–17	A very good composition demonstrating a range of musical ideas which have been developed with some imagination – appropriate to your chosen style. The selection and use of elements shows creativity.
12–14	A good composition demonstrating a range of musical ideas which have been developed competently – appropriate to your chosen style. The selection and use of elements shows some creativity.
10–11	A composition demonstrating musical ideas which have been developed satisfactorily – appropriate to your chosen style. The selection and use of elements may be simplistic and straightforward.
7–9	A composition demonstrating musical ideas which have been developed inconsistently to your chosen style. The selection and use of elements is not always appropriate.
4–6	A composition demonstrating limited musical ideas with little development appropriate to your chosen style. The selection and use of elements is poor.
1–3	A composition which shows a very limited understanding of musical ideas with no development appropriate to your chosen style. The selection and use of elements is very poor.
0	No evidence.

DON'T FORGET

You must explore and develop musical ideas using at least **four** elements from melody, harmony, rhythm, timbre and structure, one of which must be **harmony**.

THE COMPOSING REVIEW

The composing review must provide a detailed account of your composing process. It should demonstrate that you have taken care to plan your composition and that you have explored and developed ideas. You should refer specifically to the compositional methods you have used. And finally, you should reflect on your work and provide at least two specific examples of either particular strengths of your composition, or areas that think could be improved. The strengths or areas for improvement should also refer to the compositional methods you have used and how effective you think they have been developed. It is important to relate this directly to the music. General statements like *'I think my composition is effective'* or *'I could have developed some of my ideas more'* are not detailed enough.

In summary, your composing review must include a detailed account of:

- main decisions made
- exploration and development of musical ideas
- strengths and/or areas for improvement.

contd

Your composing review can be presented in prose or bullet points and as a guide should be in the region of 200 to 350 words. Short music graphics or screenshots may be included if they help to illustrate stages in the composing process. The suggested word count is given simply to indicate the overall amount of evidence required. No penalty will be applied if you are outwith this word count.

The following table shows a breakdown of the mark range from 0–10, along with the related composing review summary statements, that will be used to assess your composing review:

Mark range	Composing review summary statements
9–10	The composing review contains: • a detailed account of the main decisions made • a detailed account of the exploration and development of musical ideas • clear details of strengths and/or areas for improvement.
7–8	The composing review contains: • a fairly detailed account of the main decisions made • relevant explanation of the exploration and development of musical ideas • identification of strengths and/or areas for improvement.
5–6	The composing review contains: • a satisfactory account of the main decisions made • sufficient explanation of the exploration and development of musical ideas • a satisfactory identification of strengths and/or areas for improvement.
3–4	The composing review contains: • a limited account of the main decisions made • a limited explanation of the exploration and development of musical ideas • limited identification of strengths and/or areas for improvement.
1–2	The composing review contains: • a poor account of the main decisions made • a very limited explanation of the piece of music • little or no identification of strengths and/or areas for improvement.
0	No evidence produced.

 THINGS TO DO AND THINK ABOUT

Download a composing review template from the SQA Higher Music subject page.

Use the composing review template, with guidance notes, available at www.brightredbooks.net/HigherMusic to help structure your composing review.

 DON'T FORGET

You must use the SQA composing review template which is available from the SQA Higher Music subject page.

 ONLINE

You can also find a composing review template, with guidance notes, available at www.brightredbooks.net/HigherMusic.

PERFORMANCE 1

THE PERFORMANCE EXAM

The performance exam generally takes place in February or March, and involves you performing a programme of pieces on two instrument, or one instrument and voice, to a visiting assessor. The standard of music performed for Higher should be no less than the equivalent of Grade 4 standard of other music examining bodies (for example, ABRSM, Trinity College, London College of Music, RCS Traditional Music Grade exams etc.).

The total length of your Higher Music performance programme should be 12 minutes, and you should perform at least two contrasting pieces on each instrument, or voice. However, you can split the time of your programme any way you wish, so long as you perform at least 4 minutes on each instrument or voice. For example, you might decide to perform 6 minutes of music on each instrument. Or, you could perform 7 minutes on one and 5 minutes on the other, or 8 minutes on one and 4 minutes on the other. Just make sure that you have 12 minutes in total. If you think your programme is going to be too short, you may have to consider including an extra piece or song. If your programme turns out to be too long, you may need to consider either cutting part of the music, or fading out, as appropriate. It is not necessary to make cuts unless your total performing time is going to exceed 13 minutes, as there is some leeway allowed here. However, if you do need make cuts to any of your pieces, you must make sure that you are not lowering the standard of the piece by cutting anything from the music that makes it easier to perform.

Instrumental and vocal performances should be accompanied as appropriate. Accompaniments may be live or pre-recorded. The use of pre-recorded accompaniments or commercially-produced backing tracks is perfectly acceptable if they are stylistically appropriate.

Each piece that you play, or sing, will be marked out of 10, and then scaled to give you a mark out of 30 for each instrument. This means that your two instruments, or one instrument and voice, will be worth 60 marks. This mark will then be scaled to 50, which means that your whole performance exam is worth 50% of your overall course.

DON'T FORGET

The total length of your performance programme should be 12 minutes. Think about how you will balance the time between your two instruments, or one instrument and voice.

HOW TO PREPARE FOR THE PERFORMANCE EXAM

Try to practise regularly and reflect on your progress. Here is some advice to help you practise effectively and improve your performance.

- Practise slowly to begin with. You can build up your speed gradually and play faster when you are more confident with the music.

- Practise small sections at a time. Then work on joining up the sections you have practised.

- Focus on particular phrases or section that are causing you difficulty. Go over these slowly, making sure that you are performing accurately and fluently.

- Make sure that you are applying good technique. For instrumentalists this might include: holding the instrument, bow, sticks or beaters correctly, or using correct fingering and maintaining a good hand position. For singers this might include: paying attention to breathing, diction and communicating the meaning of the song.

- For instrumentalists and singers, you should also pay attention to musical factors such as good phrasing, dynamics and other expression marking, as well as conveying the mood and character of the music effectively.

While it is not possible to provide detailed advice on preparing for the performance exam for every single instrument, the following general advice is offered for some of the most common instrumental and vocal categories.

KEYBOARD INSTRUMENTS

Much of the advice offered here applies to all keyboard instruments (e.g. piano, electronic keyboard, electronic organ, pipe organ and accordion).

- Performances on all keyboard instruments require the use of both right and left hands.

- Performances on the piano should include attention to dynamics, phrasing and articulation, as appropriate.

- Performances on the electronic keyboard may use single-fingered or auto-chord facilities for the accompaniment.

- Performances on electronic keyboard or electronic organ may be enhanced by using changes of tone or registration, or the use of other effects such as fills, to provide variety and interest to the sound.

- Electronic organ and pipe organ performances would also benefit from changes in registration, to vary the overall sound.

A printed copy of the music you are playing needs to be provided for the visiting assessor on the day of the exam.

Music for electronic keyboard would generally consist of a melody line with chord names printed either above or below the melody. You would be expected to play the melody line with your right hand and provide the chordal accompaniment with your left hand. Music for accordion may consist of a melody line for right hand with chord names printed above or below the melody, or a fully-notated left hand part. Either would be acceptable.

DON'T FORGET

Performances on any keyboard instrument should include both right and left hands.

VOICE

As well as demonstrating both melodic and rhythmic accuracy, and attention to the same performance aspects as any other instrument, a successful vocal performance should also demonstrate very good diction and a strong sense of communicating the meaning of the song. In certain genres of popular and traditional music, it may be appropriate to interpret the music with a certain degree of melodic or rhythmic freedom. Although this can be stylistically acceptable in certain types of music, you must be careful not to interpret the song so freely that it becomes an inaccurate performance.

Singers are recommended to perform from memory, as this tends to enable a more convincing interpretation and presentation of the song. However, performing from memory is not a mandatory requirement. If you do feel that you need to rely on having a copy of the words or music, it is suggested that you place your music neatly on a music stand, to avoid the copy of the music becoming a distraction to the performance.

Songs may be accompanied or unaccompanied, as appropriate, and transposed to any suitable key. Accompaniments may be performed on any appropriate instrument. The use of pre-recorded accompaniments or commercially-produced backing tracks is perfectly acceptable if stylistically appropriate.

DON'T FORGET

Aim for good diction and a strong sense of communicating the meaning of the song.

 THINGS TO DO AND THINK ABOUT

Reflect on your performance by asking yourself the following questions.

- How accurately am I playing or singing the notes?

- How accurately am I playing or singing the rhythms?

- Am I performing the music at an appropriate and consistent tempo?

- How effectively am I conveying the mood, character and style of the music?

- To what extent am I producing a confident, convincing and well-developed tone?

- How effectively am I observing any dynamic or other expression markings?

ONLINE

Reflect on your performing progress by completing the Performance self-reflection sheet at www.brightredbooks.net/HigherMusic

85

PERFORMANCE 2

GUITAR (ACOUSTIC AND ELECTRIC) AND UKULELE

Much of the advice offered for guitar also applies to bass guitar and ukulele.

Guitar programmes may be presented in any of the following ways:

- a programme of pieces for chordal/rhythm guitar throughout
- a programme of pieces for melodic/lead guitar throughout
- a programme of pieces containing a mixture of chordal/rhythm and melodic/lead styles.

Chordal and rhythm guitar

If a guitar programme is for chordal/rhythm guitar, or a mixture of chordal/rhythm and melodic/lead styles, the programme must still contain a minimum number of 18 different chords in the performance. The chords should be played in a continuous accompanying style, which might include techniques such as strumming, finger-picking, arpeggiated chords, barré chords, or more complex playing techniques appropriate to different styles of music. Techniques might include alternating bass notes and chords, introducing runs, slurring, bending and harmonics.

In the case of a chordal/rhythm guitar piece, you need to provide a printed copy of the melodic line that the guitar is accompanying, in standard music notation. This could simply be a copy of the melody line which the chordal guitar is accompanying, with the chord names printed above or below the melody. Guitar tablature on its own is not sufficient for examination purposes. Neither is a lyric sheet with only chord names and no music notation.

The melodic line also needs to be performed, as this provides the musical context for the performance. The melodic line can be performed by your teacher, another candidate or any other performer. It could also be pre-recorded.

Electric guitar or bass guitar

If you are playing an electric guitar or bass guitar, you will have additional items of equipment to think about. As well as the instrument itself, which you will need to make sure is in tune, you will also need to make sure that you have an amplifier and a guitar lead. You may also be using an effects pedal and backing tracks. It is recommended that, before your exam, you take some time to make sure that everything you need is in full working order. It can be very unsettling to turn up for your performance exam, with your guitar and music all ready, to suddenly discover that your guitar lead isn't working, or there isn't an appropriate sound system to play your backing tracks. Here is a checklist for electric guitar and bass guitar players, to make sure that you have everything that you need for your exam.

DON'T FORGET

A Higher guitar programme featuring chordal/rhythm guitar must contain a minimum number of 18 different chords.

DON'T FORGET

A copy of the sheet music for the piece you are playing needs to be available for the visiting assessor on the day of the exam. Guitar tablature on its own is not sufficient.

PREPARING FOR THE EXAM

Before the day of the exam:

- Check that your instrument is in working order and that the strings are in good condition. It may be a good idea to have a spare set of strings to hand, just in case any break on the day.
- Check that your amplifier is working properly, and that you know what settings will suit your performance.
- Check that your guitar lead is in working order. It's always a good idea to have a spare guitar lead, just in case something goes wrong on the day.
- If you are using any additional equipment, such as an effects pedal, make sure that everything is in working order and that you have all the necessary leads.
- If you are using backing tracks to play along with, think about what media you will use to play them. For example, will your backing tracks be on a CD, or will they be MP3 files played form a phone or a computer? You will need to make sure that an appropriate sound system is available for you to be able to play your backing tracks.

contd

On the day of the exam:

- Do a final check to make sure that you have copies of the music you are playing, and all the equipment that you need.

- Make sure that all the equipment you are using, including your guitar lead, is working properly.

- Once you are set up, and ready to perform, take a minute or two to do a sound check, so that you have the correct balance in volume between your own instrument and your backing tracks. Firstly, make sure that you have the appropriate settings on your instrument, amplifier and any other equipment you will be using. Secondly, check the volume levels of any backing tracks that you are using. Make sure that the levels are suitable for both you and the visiting assessor to hear.

TUNED PERCUSSION

For performances on tuned percussion instruments, such as glockenspiel, xylophone or marimba, it is recommended that two beaters are used. While using two beaters is not a mandatory requirement, it is regarded as good practice. Although it is possible to play a piece perfectly accurately with just one beater, some pieces with melodic leaps and more complex rhythms may be difficult to perform properly without two beaters.

There are two percussion categories for SQA performance exams:

Category 1	Category 2
Drum kit	Tuned percussion:
Snare drum	Xylophone
Pipe band snare drum	Glockenspiel
Timpani	Marimba

If you select a tuned-percussion instrument from Category 2, it is also possible to offer a separate programme on an instrument from Category 1, as these instruments are in different percussion categories.

 THINGS TO DO AND THINK ABOUT

- *Guitar:* Remember to include a variety of playing techniques such as strumming, finger-picking, arpeggiated chords, barré chords, bass notes, runs, slurring, bending or harmonics within your programme.

- *Voice:* Aim to perform your vocal programme from memory, as this enables a more convincing interpretation and presentation of the song.

- *Tuned percussion:* Try to use two beaters, alternating between left and right hands. This generally results in a more accurate and fluent performance.

DON'T FORGET

If you are playing an electric guitar or bass guitar, make sure that both your amplifier and guitar lead are in good working order.

DON'T FORGET

Tuned percussion pieces should be accompanied, unless a piece is specifically an unaccompanied study.

DON'T FORGET

Accompaniments may be live or pre-recorded. The use of pre-recorded accompaniments or commercially-produced backing tracks is perfectly acceptable if stylistically appropriate.

ONLINE

Reflect on your performing progress by completing the Performance self-reflection sheet at www.brightredbooks.net/ HigherMusic

PERFORMANCE 3

DRUM KIT

For the Higher Music Performance exam, you must select and perform a complete programme on one of the following: drum kit, snare drum, pipe band snare drum or timpani (see Category 1 in Tuned percussion, page 87). It is, therefore, possible to offer a programme on a second instrument from Category 2.

For performances on drum kit, you will be required to perform a programme of pieces demonstrating five contrasting styles. You should refer to the SQA Drum kit Style Bank (see next page), and select no more than one style from any five of the nine style banks. Each style must include four different fills, and must demonstrate four-way independence (i.e. using both hands and both feet).

Accompaniments

Drum kit programmes must be accompanied, to provide a musical context for the performance. Accompaniments for drum kit programmes can be either live or pre-recorded. The use of pre-recorded accompaniments or commercially-produced backing tracks is perfectly acceptable if stylistically appropriate. However, it is also acceptable for one drum kit piece only within the whole programme to be unaccompanied.

Styles

It is also possible, in a drum kit programme, to include two styles within the one piece (e.g. Rock and Disco). However, this is only permitted within one piece in the programme. In this case it would not be necessary to include double the number of fills.

HOW TO PREPARE FOR THE PERFORMANCE EXAM

Useful advice

Drum kit candidates should be aware that some commercially-available drum kit publications, although produced for particular graded examinations, may not always contain the appropriate number of fills required for SQA examinations. If you use such publications, you may need to include extra fills at appropriate places in the music in order to meet the SQA requirements. Such additional fills would need to be notated on the copy of the music.

If your drum kit programme is too long, it is perfectly acceptable to make cuts, or fade-out (in the case of backing-tracks) as appropriate, to keep within the time limit. However, if you do make cuts to the music, or fade-out before the end, you must make sure that you are still including all the appropriate requirements in terms of styles, fills and four-way independence.

DON'T FORGET

A Higher drum kit programme must contain five contrasting styles (from the Style Bank). Each style must include four different fills, and must demonstrate four-way independence.

In selecting five contrasting styles, drum kit candidates should also be aware that some commercially-available drum kit publications may contain pieces that don't necessarily relate to the rhythm style suggested in the title of the piece. For example, you might be playing a piece called *Bright Red Blues*, suggesting that the piece would in a **Blues** style (from Style Bank 3). However, although the piece may be based on a **Blues** chord progression, it might actually use a **Rock** rhythm (from Style Bank 1). It is very important, therefore, to make sure that the five rhythm styles that you include in your drum kit programme all come from different Style Banks.

contd

SQA Drum kit Style Bank

Bank 1	Bank 2	Bank 3	Bank 4	Bank 5	Bank 6	Bank 7	Bank 8	Bank 9
Rock Heavy Rock Rock Ballad Metal Rock	Disco 16th note rhythm	Blues (3 quavers to one crotchet)	Shuffle	Jazz (2 or 4 feel)	Waltz	Reggae	Cha Cha	Irregular Time Signatures
Pop	16 beat	12/8	Funk shuffle	Swing	3 beats (Simple or Compound Time)	Ska	Bossa Nova	Free choice of any other style not listed in Banks 1–8
Hip hop Soul Hard Rock Punk Funk R'n'B Rock'n'roll				Big Band Swing	9/8		Latin Samba Rumba Calypso	

DON'T FORGET

For Higher Music you must perform five contrasting styles from five different style banks.

ORCHESTRAL INSTRUMENTS

If you are playing an orchestral instrument, one important factor to keep in mind for your performance exam is to make sure that your instrument is properly in tune. It is perfectly acceptable to have your teacher tune the instrument for you.

While you may be playing an unaccompanied piece as part of your programme, such as an unaccompanied study, it is likely that most of your programme will require some form of accompaniment. The accompaniment may be live, played on the piano or some other instrument, or pre-recorded. You may use a commercially-produced backing track for your accompaniment if this is stylistically appropriate. If your accompaniment is going to be live, make sure that you have adequate time to rehearse with your accompanist. It may be that your own instrumental teacher will accompany you, meaning that you will probably have had many opportunities to practise with the accompaniment in your lessons. However, if someone else is going to accompany you, it would be advisable for you to make arrangements with them, well in advance of the exam, to allow both of you adequate time to rehearse together.

DON'T FORGET

Make sure your instrument is in tune.

DON'T FORGET

Allow yourself plenty of time to rehearse with your accompanist.

 THINGS TO DO AND THINK ABOUT

Is your backing/accompaniment going to be a live performance, pre-recorded backing tracks, or a mixture of both?

Make sure that you give yourself plenty of time to practise with the appropriate backing/accompaniment.

 ONLINE

Reflect on your performing progress by completing the Performance self-reflection sheet at www.brightredbooks.net/HigherMusic

PERFORMANCE 4

BAGPIPES

Highland bagpipes must be presented for the Higher Music performance exam. A practice chanter would not be acceptable.

Bagpipe candidates are required to perform their bagpipe programme from memory. There is no requirement to play a March, Strathspey *and* Reel. The emphasis is on performing a varied programme of contrasting styles.

It is current practice for bagpipe candidates to be assessed by a specialist bagpipe visiting assessor. This means that your bagpipe performance exam will most likely be on a different day from the performance exam for your other instrument, or voice.

TRADITIONAL MUSIC PERFORMANCES

The general advice offered here is for instruments such as Scots fiddle, tin whistle, clarsach accordion and voice, performing traditional music.

While a number of performers who play or sing traditional music learn a lot of their music *by ear*, it is still a requirement of the SQA performance exam that a copy of the printed music must be provided for the visiting assessor.

In many cases this shouldn't pose too much difficulty, as there are a number of publications of Traditional songs and Fiddle tunes that could be used for examination purposes. The Royal Conservatoire of Scotland also publishes a range of appropriate pieces for the Traditional Music Graded Exams.

If, however, you are performing a traditional tune that you do not have the sheet music for, you may need to create your own printed version of the melody. You could do this either by writing the melody out on manuscript paper, or by using music notation software to produce your own sheet music version of the piece. Even if you do have a copy of the sheet music, you may be performing your own interpretation of the music or embellishing the melody. In this case it would be advisable to annotate your copy of the music to show exactly what you are doing.

As is the case with some styles of popular music, it can be acceptable to interpret some Traditional tunes with a certain degree of melodic or rhythmic freedom. Although this can be stylistically appropriate, you must be careful not to interpret the piece so freely that it does not actually relate well to the printed music. In this case your performance may be regarded as inaccurate.

Useful advice

Keep in mind the following points when preparing for your exam:

- *Bagpipes:* There is no requirement to play a March, Strathspey *and* Reel. Consider performing a varied programme of contrasting styles.
- *Traditional music performances:* While it is stylistically acceptable to perform sets of traditional pieces (like Scots fiddle tunes) unaccompanied, it may be helpful to have a piano playing a vamp accompaniment. This can help to keep the tempo and flow appropriate and consistent. Make sure that you give yourself plenty of time to practise with the appropriate accompaniment.

ASSESSMENT OF PERFORMANCE

On the day of your performance exam a visiting assessor will listen to your full programme and mark each piece individually out of 10. In order to award you a mark, they will consider how well your overall performance of each piece relates to a number of performance aspects, as well as considering how well your performance meets the performance summary statements.

DON'T FORGET

Bagpipe candidates are required to perform their programme from memory.

DON'T FORGET

As with all styles of music, you will need to provide a printed copy of the music for the performance exam.

ONLINE

Reflect on your performing progress by completing the Performance self-reflection sheet at www.brightredbooks.net/HMusic

contd

The following table shows the different performance aspects that will be used in assessing your performance of each piece. It also provides a summary of the criteria you should be aiming for within each performance aspect, as well as some common faults that you should be trying to avoid.

Performance aspect	Criteria that you should be aiming for:	Some common faults to be avoided:
Melodic accuracy/ intonation	Notes performed correctly, as written in the music. Playing or singing in tune.	Notes not performed correctly according to the music. Playing or singing is not in tune.
Rhythmic accuracy	Rhythms performed correctly, as written in the music.	Rhythms not performed correctly according to the music.
Tempo and flow	Keeping in time and performing fluently. Performing at an appropriate and consistent tempo. A musically convincing performance.	Not keeping properly in time. Some faltering or stumbling. Performing at an inappropriate or inconsistent tempo. Breaks in continuity.
Mood and character	Conveying the mood, character and style of the music appropriately. Communicating the meaning of the music or song with sensitivity. Paying attention to musical details and expression.	Not conveying the mood, character or style of the music appropriately. Not communicating the meaning of the music or song effectively. Paying little or no attention to musical details or expression.
Tone	Producing a good tone. A confident, convincing and well-developed instrumental or vocal sound. On the keyboard: using different tones, fills or effects.	Tone quality not good. Little evidence of development or control of the instrumental or vocal sound. Not changing tone, or using other effects such as fills.
Dynamics	Paying attention to dynamic markings in the printed music. Varying the volume level.	Not observing dynamic markings in the music. No variation in volume.

The following table shows a breakdown of the mark range from 0–10, along with the related performance summary statements, that will be used to assess your performance:

Mark range	Performance summary statements
9–10	A convincing and stylish performance which demonstrates excellent technique.
7–8	A secure performance musically and technically.
5–6	A mainly accurate performance displaying effective technical and musical control.
3–4	An inconsistent performance lacking sufficient technical and/or musical skill to communicate the sense of the music.
0–2	A poor performance with little or no evidence of required technical and/or musical ability.

After each piece that you play has been marked out of 10, the individual marks are then scaled to give you a mark out of 30 for each instrument. This means that your two instruments, or one instrument and voice, will be worth 60 marks. This mark will then be scaled to 50, which means that your whole performance exam is worth 50% of your overall course.

 THINGS TO DO AND THINK ABOUT

Consider a piece that you are currently playing or singing:

- Think about how your performance currently relates to the different performance aspects. Which of the performance summary statements would best describe your performance overall?

- Think about how well your performance would meet the criteria that you should be aiming for. What could you do to improve your performance?

APPENDICES

GLOSSARY OF CONCEPTS

Accent When a note or chord is given more attack or emphasised. In music notation, this is indicated by a small arrowhead either above or below the note:

Acciaccatura A **grace note**. A type of ornament played as a short, 'crushed note', before the main note of a melody. In music notation *acciaccaturas* are usually printed in smaller type as a quaver with a diagonal line cutting through it:

Added 6th A basic three note chord with the 6th note above the root added. For example, if a 6th was added the chords of C, F or G, they would become C6, F6 and G6:

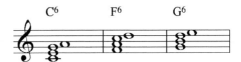

Augmentation When the note values of a melody are lengthened, usually by doubling the value.

Bass clef notes The notes on the *bass clef* range from low E (on the ledger line below the stave) to middle C (on the ledger line above the stave):

Basso continuo Sometimes referred to just as *continuo*. In Baroque music, the continuo part consists of a bass line (*basso continuo*) usually played by a cello. A chordal instrument such as a harpsichord, organ or lute would fill in harmonies over the bass line. Sometimes figures are written under the bass line indicating the chords to be played. This is called figured bass.

Cadence A harmonic progression of at least two chords that come at the end of a phrase, section, or complete piece of music. See *Plagal cadence* and *Interrupted cadence*.

Chamber music Music composed for a small group, generally intended to be performed in a palace chamber or large room rather than a large concert hall. See *String quartet*.

Chords I, IV, V and VI in major and minor keys in treble and bass clefs. These are chords based on the 1st, 4th, 5th and 6th notes of the scale.

Key	Chord I, V, IV and VI in the treble clef	Chord I, V, IV and VI in the bass clef
C major		
G major		
F major		
A minor		

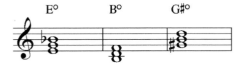

Coloratura A type of operatic voice that features florid ornamentation, elaborate melodic decoration and runs. Although the term can be applied to any type of voice, it is most often associated with the *soprano*.

Concertino The small group of solo instruments in a *concerto grosso*. See *Concerto grosso* and *Ripieno*.

Concerto grosso A type of concerto, common in Baroque music, in which a group of soloists (*concertino*) is combined and contrasted with a larger group of strings (*ripieno*). See *Ripieno* and *Concertino*.

Continuo See *Basso continuo*.

Crotchet rest See *Rests*.

Da capo (D.C.) Italian term indicating that the performer should repeat a piece of music from the beginning. The abbreviation is **D.C.**

Da capo aria An *aria* in *Ternary* form (A B A), found in *opera* and *oratorio* in the 17th and 18th centuries, in which third section is not written out but the instruction *Da capo* (from the beginning) is given instead. The singer would then vary or embellish the melody on the return to section A.

D.C. Abbreviation for *Da capo*. See *Da capo*.

Diminished triad A three-note chord consisting to two intervals of a minor 3rd built on top of each other. Here are examples of *diminished triads* based on E, B and G sharp, using common abbreviations:

Diminished 7th A chord consisting of three intervals of a minor 3rd built one on top of the other, the interval between the lower and top note being a diminished 7th. Here are examples of *diminished 7th* chords based on E, B and G sharp, using common abbreviations:

Diminution When the note values of a melody are shortened, usually by halving the value.

Dominant The note or chord based on the 5th note of a scale. See the **Music Literacy** section.

Dominant 7th A chord built on the *dominant* (5th note of a scale) with the lowered 7th note added above its root. In the key of C major the dominant 7th chord would be G7 (containing the notes G, B, D and F) because G is the dominant (5th) note. Here are examples of dominant 7th chords based on C, F and G:

Dotted crotchet rest See *Rests*.

Exposition The first section of a movement in *sonata form,* containing two musical themes called the *first subject* and the *second subject*. See *Sonata form* and *Subject*.

Harmonic minor scale The minor scale which shares the same key signature as its *Relative major* with the 7th note raised by a semitone. The *harmonic minor scale* is exactly the same both ascending and descending:

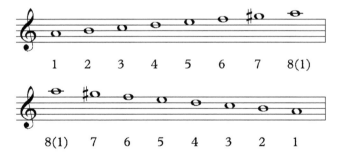

See *Melodic minor scale*.

Harmonics The very high, faint notes (called overtones), produced on a bowed string instrument, or guitar, by lightly touching the strings at certain points. On a guitar these can sound bell-like.

Impressionist A 20th-century style which makes use of *pentatonic scales* and *whole-tone scales*, *discords* and *chromatic* harmonies, and fluid rhythms with a vague sense of pulse. The term is borrowed from a style of painting in which the images were often blurred and hazy.

Interrupted cadence A chord progression formed by chords V–VI. In the key of C major this would be the chord of G major followed by the chord of A minor. This is also sometimes referred to as a 'surprise' cadence as the listener may be expecting V–I which would sound more final.

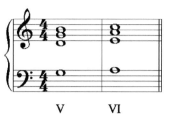

See *Cadence* and *Plagal cadence*

Interval The distance in pitch between two notes, e.g. C-D is a 2nd, C-E is a 3rd, C–F is a 4th, C-G is a 5th, C-A is a 6th, C-B is a 7th and low C-high C is an octave:

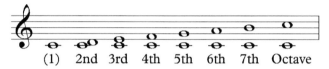

See the **Music Literacy** section for examples of intervals in different keys.

Irregular time signatures Time signatures that are not in *simple* or *compound time*. *Irregular time signatures* often have five or seven beats in every bar.

Jazz funk A style that combines *Jazz improvisation* with elements of *Rock* and Funk. Common features include the use of amplified instruments such as synthesizers, electric guitars, bass guitar and drum kit, along with Funk influenced bass lines and the driving rhythms and character of Rock.

Lied German word for song – refers to works for solo voice and piano by German composers of the Romantic period in which the voice and piano are equally important. The text would be in German and the structure of the verses would either *strophic* or *through-composed*. See *Through-composed*.

Mass A religious choral work, usually sung in Latin, comprising five main sections:
Kyrie eleison, Christe eleison
Gloria in excelcis Deo
Credo in unum deum
Sanctus; Osanna; Benedictus
Agnus Dei

Melodic minor scale The minor scale which shares the same key signature as its *relative major* and has the 6th and 7th notes raised by a semitone when ascending, and lowered when descending:

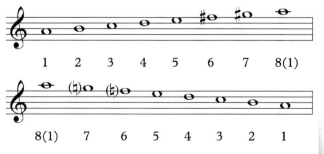

See *Harmonic minor scale*.

Minim rest See *Rests*.

Modal A term used to describe music based on a *mode*, a type of scale commonly found in *plainchant*. *Modes* are also found in folk music and are also used in *jazz* and popular styles of music. See *Mode* and *Plainchant*.

Mode An early type of scale, often used as the basis of folk song melodies and *plainchant*. See *Modal*. Here is the *Dorian mode* (all the white notes on the keyboard between low D and high D):

Mordent An ornament which sounds the main note, the note above and then the main note again. An inverted mordent sounds the main note, the note below and then the main note again. An upper *mordent* would be notated like this:

 and performed like this:

Musique concrète A 20th century style that makes use of recorded natural sounds, which are modified using editing techniques such as cutting and re-assembling, playing backwards, slowing down and speeding up. Some composers have combined *Musique concrète* techniques with electronic sounds or acoustic instruments.

Obbligato A prominent and important instrumental *countermelody* in a piece of vocal music.

Oratorio A large-scale musical work for SATB chorus, soloists and orchestra, based on a religious story often taken from the Bible. Like an *opera*, an *oratorio* features *recitatives, arias,* and *choruses*. However, unlike an *opera*, it would be performed without costumes or scenery.

Passacaglia A form/structure in which a repeating bass line, usually with 3 beats in the bar and in a minor key, is the main theme heard below varying textures and harmonies. Similar to a *ground bass*.

Phrase mark A curved line indicating that a particular group of notes are linked together to form part of a melody:

Plagal cadence A chord progression formed by chords IV-I. In the key of C major this would be the chord of F major followed by the chord of C major. This is also sometimes referred to as the 'amen' cadence as it is often used at the end of hymn tunes.

IV   I

See *Cadence* and *Interrupted cadence*.

Plainchant An early style of church music sometimes referred to as *Plainsong* or *Gregorian chant,* consisting of a single line, unaccompanied vocal melody with Latin words. *Plainchant* is generally *modal* and has no regular metre. See *Mass, Mode,* and *Modal*.

Quaver rest See *Rests*.

Recitative A vocal piece where the music follows the natural rhythm of speech. It is used in *operas* and *oratorios* to move the story or plot on. A *recitative* usually leads into an *aria* or a *chorus*.

Relative major A major key related to a minor key that shares the same key signature. The relative major key can be found by going to the 3rd note of the minor scale. For example, C major is the relative major of A minor. A piece of music in a minor key will sometime modulate to the *relative major*. See *Relative minor*.

Relative minor A minor key related to a major key that shares the same key signature. The relative minor key can be found by going to the 6th note of the major scale. For example, A minor is the relative minor of C major. A piece of music in a major key will sometime modulate to the *relative minor*. See *Relative major*.

Rests A silence in music. Every note value in music has a corresponding sign (called a *rest*) indicating the equivalent length of silence. The table shows common *rests*, along with the corresponding notes, and the number of beats each note and rest lasts for.

Note	Name	Length	Rest
𝅝	Semibreve	4 beats	▬
𝅗𝅥.	Dotted minim	3 beats	▬.
𝅗𝅥	Minim	2 beats	▬
𝅘𝅥.	Dotted crotchet	1 ½ beats	𝄽. or 𝄾..
𝅘𝅥	Crotchet	1 beat	𝄽 or 𝄾
𝅘𝅥𝅮	Quaver	½ beat	𝄿

Ripieno The large group of string instruments found in a *concerto grosso*. See *Concerto grosso* and *Concertino*.

Ritornello A form, common in Baroque music, in which a recurring theme alternates with other contrasting themes called episodes. In a *Concerto grosso,* the *ritornello* is the recurring theme played by the *ripieno* group (the orchestra) and sometimes by *concertino* group (the soloists). The *ritornello* theme may return several times throughout a movement. Similar to a *Rondo*. See *Concerto grosso*.

Semibreve rest See *Rests*.

Slur A curved line indicating that a particular group of notes should be played smoothly (legato), without separation:

Sonata A piece of music for one or two instruments, usually in three or four movements. **Sonatas** are often composed for solo piano or another instrument with piano accompaniment.

Sonata form Sometimes known as 'first movement' form. The term is used to describe the structure of the first movement of **sonatas,** *symphonies* and **string quartets**. A movement structured in **sonata form** has tthree main sections: *exposition, development* and *recapitulation*. The **exposition** introduces two contrasting themes in related keys called the *first* **subject** and the *second* **subject**. See **Exposition** and **subject**.

Soul A style of Afro-American popular music which includes elements of *blues* and *gospel* and conveys strong emotions.

String quartet This term can be used in two slightly different ways, depending on the context. As well as describing the group of performers that make up a **string quartet** (*timbre*) it can also describe the type of music played by a **string quartet** (*style*).

Timbre: a group of four instruments comprising two violins, viola and cello.

Style: a piece of music composed for a **string quartet**, often in three or four movements.

Subdominant The note or chord based on the 4th note of a scale. See the **Music Literacy** section.

Subject The main theme or melody, or group of musical ideas, in a piece of music. The two main themes in **sonata form** are called the *first* **subject** and the *second* **subject**. See **Sonata form** and **Exposition**.

Staccato Italian term indicating that a note or chord is to be played short and detached. In music notation this is indicated by a dot either above or below the note:

Three against two (3 against 2). One part, or line, of music playing in groups of three, while at the same time another part would be playing in groups of two. For example, one part might be playing *quavers* while the other part plays **triplet quavers**, or one part might be playing *crotchets* while the other part plays **triplet crotchets**. You can see examples of three against two in *Mad Rush* for piano by Philip Glass and in the following extract from *Arabesque No. 1* for piano by Debussy.

See **Triplets**, **Triplet crotchets** and **Triplet quavers**.

Time changes A term used to identify a change in time signature. For example, a change from 3 beats in the bar to 4 beats in the bar. You can see an example of time changes in the opening of *Intermezzo Interrotto* from *Concerto for Orchestra* by Bartok.

Tonic The note or chord based on the 1st note of a scale. See the **Music Literacy** section.

Through-composed The structure of a song in which there is little or no repetition of music for each verse.

Tierce de Picardie A major chord heard at the end of a piece of music in a minor key.

Tremolando An Italian term that describes either a rapidly repeated note (particularly the rapid up-and-down movement of a bow on a stringed instrument), or the rapid alternation between two different notes at least a 3rd apart.

Triplet crotchets A group of three crotchets played in the time of two, shown is music notation as:

See **Triplets**, **Triplet quavers** and **Three against two (3 against 2).**

Triplet quavers A group of three quavers played in the time of two, shown is music notation as:

See **Triplets**, **Triplet crotchets** and **Three against two (3 against 2)**

Triplets A group of three notes played in the time of two. The sign in music notation to indicate **triplets** is the number *3* written either above or below the middle note. A square bracket, or sometimes a curved line (like a slur), may also be added to indicate the notes forming the **triplet** rhythm. See **Triplet quavers**, **Triplet crotchets** and **Three against two (3 against 2)**.

Whole bar rest See **Rests**.

INDEX